Lonely Planet

YOU ONLY LIVE ONCE

A LIFETIME OF ADVENTURES FOR THE EXPLORER IN ALL OF US

"YOU ONLY LIVE ONCE; BUT IF YOU DO IT RIGHT, ONCE IS ENOUGH"

– MAE WEST

CONTENTS

AN HOUR

In which we spend a couple
of hours taking care of the
little things – a swim, a
shower, perhaps a cocktail
or a movie – before
tackling the big stuff:
extreme feats, life-and-
death spectacles, celestial
phenomena and the ever-
thought-provoking rituals
of dawn and sunset.

A DAY

In which we lose ourselves
at festivals and carnivals,
dine like kings, party
all night in cities and
fall asleep in some
extraordinary settings.
Then we spend a day
or two in the outdoors,
watching wildlife, exploring
by moonlight and seeking
out the most silent places
in the world. Finally, we
face our greatest fears,
whatever they may be.

A WEEK

130-185

In which we take a week or two to drive the world's most exciting roads, spot the Big Five on safari, dive into lost worlds and visit the backdrops to favourite fictional scenes. Closer to home, a week is time enough to discover delights on your doorstep and learn some dance steps to impress.

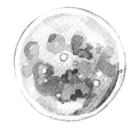

A MONTH

186-233

In which, over a month or more, we follow in the footsteps of great women, take voyages without flying, travel from one end of a country to the other, train for a marathon and let our inner child take charge. We also find time to volunteer and travel solo. And to escape it all, we seek solace in a retreat or a remote cabin in the woods.

A YEAR

234-279

In which we live and work on the road, learn to freedive, join an intrepid scientific research mission, travel in memory of a loved one, and resolve to learn a new language. Then, consider working on a yacht or becoming a ski instructor, or even taking a round-the-world journey with the perfect travel companion.

INTRODUCTION

'Life's not a dress rehearsal.' 'Carpe Diem.' 'Be happy while you're living for you're a long time dead.' Yes, there are a lot of motivational proverbs about living life to the max out there, including the title of this book. But that's probably because it's a big deal.

There's a lot to pack in. Some people are born with a knack for sucking the marrow from the bones of life. And that's what the second edition of this book sets out to help you do. It is not just another bucketlist of big-ticket trips. We've all heard about Venice and, yes, it is probably worth going to Italy to see its waterways. Instead, hopefully you'll take away something more from this book: a resolve to live life to the fullest, to add a dash of *joie de vivre* to every day.

That doesn't just mean splashing out on exotic holidays but also seeking out and indulging in little pleasures – a night at the museum spent drifting off beneath a cabinet of ancient wonders; an afternoon delighting in a seasonal tasting menu at one of the world's best restaurants. And, while we feature a number of serious challenges – trekking Mount Fuji (left), it's worth noting, doesn't get any easier the older you grow – there are just as many experiences that you can enjoy on your doorstep with a little lateral thinking.

Start by embracing spontaneity; experiences like wild camping under the stars, once in a while, remind you what an amazing privilege it is to be alive, to think and to enjoy the world around us.

And we've tried to suggest opportunities to learn and slake a little of that thirst for knowledge among these pages, with illustrations of how to mix cocktails, identify autumn leaves and train for a marathon with a difference. For hedonists and adventure-lovers we've also mapped once-in-a-lifetime experiences in cities and on islands.

Essentially, You Only Live Once is about
experiences, responsible travel and giving back to a
planet that needs our care – not simply ticking off
places to visit – though we travel to every corner of the
globe. It is about those experiences that you will replay
in your mind's eye years later; they may not feature
the most spectacular destinations, they may even
in fact have cost nothing, but they will be the travel
experiences that changed you and those around you, the
ones that still bring a smile to your face.

So, how does this book work? There are five chapters
– for an Hour, Day, Week, Month and Year – and in each
we suggest experiences that may take about that amount
of time. Naturally, these definitions are as elastic as you
want them to be; you can stretch a day into a weekend,
a week into a fortnight. You can spend one month or six
working remotely abroad as a digital nomad or in local
regenerative outreaches, or take a year or more to travel
around the world.

But what all these ideas have in common is that
they're starting points. They will reignite long-forgotten
desires – to learn a craft or a language or get back to
nature – or spark new and unexpected ambitions: why
shouldn't you live out of a van for a year?

When you know what's stopping you, you can start
working on a solution. Perhaps this book will be as useful
in helping you identify obstacles as will be for refining
your month's or your year's travel experiences. Then it's
time to turn to Lonely Planet's extensive travel resources
– from a community of new and inspiring voices – and
begin planning the rest of your life.

CHAPTER 1

AN HOUR

BE
PRESENT

Whether it's an improv solo at a late-night gig in a New York jazz club or a show of natural majesty such as an annual meteor shower like the Leonids, there's no better way of appreciating the experience than putting away any tech devices and being present in the moment.

WITNESS THE DAWN

The sun comes up every day, yet always has the power to astonish: it's the combination of a slow-burn then sudden illumination. Picture getting up at stupid o'clock to witness the first light spreading in picture-book panorama. You reach the perfect perch and wait. First the sky's seams seem to tear, a fraying at the edge of the darkness. It turns navy, then paler blue. Purple-pinks warm the horizon. Then the sun bursts in. The world's best alarm clock has rung; what lies ahead is fresh possibility.

1

Mt Sinai
Egypt

The mountain is easy and beautiful to climb, and offers a taste of the magnificence of southern Sinai's high mountain region. For pilgrims, it also shares a moving glimpse into biblical times. If touring from Sharm El Sheikh you can see the sun rise over the ancient landscape from the summit, and still arrive back at the base in time to visit St Catherine's Monastery as it opens for the day.

Essential information:
Mt Sinai climbers must be accompanied by local Bedouin guides, who can be hired from the monastery car park.

2

Dzibilchaltún
Mexico

Twice a year, at sunrise on the spring and autumn equinoxes, the sun truly shines here at Dzibilchaltún, which lies about 17km (10 miles) due north of central Mérida. The sunlight beams directly between the doorposts of the Temple of the Seven Dolls – testament to the architectural mastery of the Maya. Witness the temple doors glowing in the sunlight, then watch them light up as the sun passes behind them and casts a cool square beam across the crumbling walls.

Essential information:
Equinox sunrises fall on approximately March 20 and September 22.

3

Gisborne
New Zealand

The North Island's easternmost city is the first big hub to see the sun rise. It's also within one of the few districts that permits 'freedom camping'; all year round you can wild-camp in a vehicle away from the crowds and watch the new day dawn over the Pacific. Choose between Midway Beach, Kaiti Beach, Bright St, Makorori, Tokomaru Bay or Motu. Explore the historic wharf at 'Toko', spot roaming kiwi after dusk or trek through native forests of the Whinray Scenic Reserve Track.

Essential information:
It's a three-night maximum stay, and you'll need to be sleeping in a self-contained vehicle in the designated parking areas.

4

Longyearbyen
Svalbard, Norway

At 78 degrees north, Norway's Svalbard region is the largest continuous wilderness in Europe, and the final frontier before the North Pole. Svalbard's capital, Longyearbyen, is the only town of any size, and acts a portal to the magical white wonderland. Polar night – when the sun doesn't rise above the horizon – lasts for over four months on this Arctic archipelago. The first time the sun makes an appearance in Longyearbyen (around 8 March) is special indeed.

Essential information:
Flights operate regularly between Oslo and Longyearbyen.

SUNRISE AT SUMMER SOLSTICE

Dan Fahey seeks connection at Stonehenge's dawn gathering.

Where do you go to feel something? After months of overwork and under-sleep, I was exhausted. My downtime was filled with thumbing through social media or reading newspapers. Novels piled unread next to my bed. Dates with mates were made – and then routinely missed. My empathy was empty. I needed to do something to stimulate my brain and kickstart my heart.

Walking along England's chalk cliffs in East Sussex, the sea wind whipping into my face, an idea came to me: to reconnect with life, I should watch the sunrise at Britain's most famous prehistoric monument, Stonehenge. I don't know why I thought this mystic collection of rocks – some dragged over 160km (100 miles) from Pembrokeshire to Wiltshire – would be the remedy I needed, but I wanted to be phone-free and actually feel something.

That something would either be the lashing summer rain that this part of England sometimes endures, or the majesty of the sun arcing up over the horizon on the longest day of the year, illuminating this mathematically-aligned megalith in the same way it did 5000 years ago.

This could give me a direct line to 2500 BCE. It could allow me to have an identical experience to that of my forebears, back when they were part of the natural world, rather than trying to control it.

From Egypt to Ireland and Malta to Mexico, civilizations from across the globe and spanning many aeons have built great monuments to pay deference to the sun. Could watching that big ball of life-giving fire rise up in the sky make me feel alive again? Either way, it had to be better than scrolling past another tweet, right?

Some old university friends and I caught the train to Salisbury and arrived around lunchtime. The station was packed, buzzing with cosmic energy: wrinkled hippie couples; families shouting noisily; a glut of students wearing tie-dyed, Aladdin-style trousers and patchwork hoodies. After disembarking a shuttle bus we began the 2.4km (1.5-mile) uphill trudge toward the stones. A sort of skittish jollity echoed through the crowd, powered by some Celtic-sounding music being pumped out of speakers in wheelbarrows.

There's usually a fence protecting the hallowed sarsens themselves, but during the summer solstice visitors can enter the circle and touch the very same silcrete rock and bluestone that their pagan ancestors hauled up here thousands of years ago.

Cold and smooth, the stones exude an all-knowing calm. Laid out along the solstitial axis, there is an outer circle of stones and an inner horseshoe-shaped curve of bluestones. In the middle are the trilithons, where a horizontal lintel is held up by two upright stones.

Spilling out across the green earthwork enclosures were a number of pulsing drum circles, each hammering out a hypnotic rhythm. Dum-dum-dum-dum, dum-dum-dum-dum. The sun soon set, making way for a cold, cloudless night. As we danced with strangers, the stars seemed to shine brighter.

The hours passed and more people arrived. The drummers went nuts, they sped up, and I genuinely lost myself in a farrago of frolicking that lasted until first light. Two hours felt like five minutes.

Eventually, everyone headed to the eastern face of the circle to welcome the sun. A purple mist covered the stones and the dew on the horizon shimmered. A coven of witches cast their own ceremonial circle away from the murmuring hoards; I went and joined them and asked what they were about to do.

'A ceremony to cast spells,' said Tree, a death doula and Wicca witch. 'We're calling on the sun's alchemical energy to burn away things that don't serve us any more. The elemental energy of the sun is also a great catalyst, motivator and activator – purpose and passion will be born.'

And that's exactly why I was here. This wasn't a bacchanalian bop in a field: we were here to give thanks, in our own way, to that great giver of life in the sky. The witches started to burn rosemary to cleanse the space and then meditated on what they wanted to 'activate'. They created a 'cone of power', lifting their arms up to the centre of the circle to draw down the energy of the sun. I felt gloriously out of my comfort zone, but their purpose was as pure as mine: we both leaned into a moment of mindfulness that honoured the fact that we were alive.

'Isn't it amazing we're on this planet right now,' said Tree. 'It's like winning the best lottery.'

But money doesn't buy you this: the sun slowly rose above the Heel Stone, casting a long shadow that grew up and across the field, entering a stone trilithon on the outer circle.

People cheered, there were primaeval roars. Midsummer was upon us. The shadow then entered the inner circle and went into the Altar Stone. As soon as it hit, the sun came up, the shadow disappeared and this generation of revellers was bathed in the gold of the sun.

That warmth stayed with me all summer. I could feel again.

TO THE SEA

Adam Skolnick finds solace
swimming in California's open ocean.

The colours soothe me. To be immersed in aquamarine water marinates the mind, opens it up and hushes my restless brain. I'll see JM's bubbles sometimes, the wake of his shallow kicks foaming white on the glassy surface.

Glinting balls of silver sardines swirl as we approach the rock reef just off Point Dume in Malibu, the stones crusted with spiny blue urchins and sprawling lavender starfish. There are striped bass and bright orange garibaldi, and when the sun is high, white bolts bounce off the sandy bottom, forming an underwater sundial.

We explore thick kelp forests, take deep nourishing breaths and follow the billowing light-green foliage to the floor. We slalom the giant stalks that recall a magic-beans fairy tale. Even on bright days, it's dark in the forest, patched together with sandy meadows saturated in turquoise light. I'll strain to make it all the way there and surface to deep breaths of relief, while waves thrash the sandstone cliffs and the sun glistens gold on the tides.

On winter days we'll emerge on the beach shivering, our hands blue, teeth chattering. In the summer we'll stroll back to our starting point in the sun, warm and alive. We always laugh about something. No matter what else is going on in our lives, when the ocean has done its work, we always smile.

It took years for JM to get me in the water – and I had always previously had an excuse. Then came the summer of 2012. The Mayan apocalypse may never have materialised, but my personal apocalypse arrived right on time. I seriously injured my back and could no longer run. Couldn't even sit. The pain stayed with me for months. I was just 40 years old, and I couldn't move as well as most 70-year-olds. And it wasn't just my back that was wrecked: my marriage was on the verge of collapse. It was as if the emotional weight I was carrying was too much for my physiology, and eventually everything blew up at once.

In the midst of the collapse, I met a clever massage therapist from northern Thailand, and she demanded I get in the water. So I found a pool at a nearby community college, and my back started to loosen. My lungs started working again, my body felt strong for the first time in forever. But there was no wild-nature love in the pool. There was never a deeper meaning.

JM called one day. I told him I was swimming and he convinced me to give the ocean a try. It was August. The water was 19°C (66°F) – warm enough to enjoy. The sea was crystal. We counted more than 50 bull rays gliding along the sandy bottom. After the swim, JM started talking about the positive ions, and how they funnel positivity into our cells by osmosis, or something. False or true, I was willing to believe. In those early days, the swim was the only good thing in my life.

Since then I've swum with groups of sea lions 20-strong, with super-pods of dolphins; I've mingled with migrating whales. We'll swim in stormy seas, navigate head-high surf and ride heavy currents sparked by swirling winds that lure in the kitesurfers. Sometimes we'll swim only a metre from one another and not make eye contact for a mile, each of us hidden in the trough of great swells.

We'll swim in soupy fog, we'll swallow bellyfuls of blue water, watch flocks of pelicans skim the sea in formation. We've made friends with – and occasionally frightened – the lifeguards, who think we're mad. One confessed that he feels scared out by the rock reef: 'I prefer being at the top of the food chain.'

We know great white sharks patrol here, though we've never seen one. Occasionally they cross my mind

on murky cold-water days, when we're outfitted like seals in our wetsuits. But usually I swim free and easy.

JM likes to tell a story about the 80-somethings he occasionally swims with at La Jolla Cove. There are a group of about a dozen of these wise old masters – men and women who gather to swim year-round, without wetsuits. As JM was preparing to go out, one of those ladies came out of the drink with a goofy smile on her face. A bystander sipping coffee approached her and asked how it was.

'Amazing!' she said.

'Was there good visibility?' the bystander asked.

'Oh no, couldn't see anything out there.'

'Was it warm?'

'It was freezing,' said the swimmer. She was towel-drying and shivering by then.

'But you liked it?' asked the confused bystander.

'It was amazing!' she said, beaming gloriously. JM plans to be just like her one day. Me too.

TAKE
A BATH

Hot or cold, clothed or not, nothing washes away the day like immersing yourself in a bath. Hungarians have long known this, and the baths at the Gellert Hotel in Budapest are just one of several grand indoor and outdoor bathing spots in Hungary's capital. In volcanic Japan, steaming hot springs (onsens) are just as much part of the culture. Prefer a cold dip? Head to Finland in winter when 170 ice-holes are open for a post-sauna shock.

HARNESS THE WIND

From dreams about flight to wacky winged apparatus, humans have long been gripped by the yearning to fly. There are centuries of failed flying machines behind us, like Leonardo da Vinci's wing-flapping ornithopter and the notorious 'Artificial Albatross', but finally we cracked the code. There's now a multitude of mid-air modes of transport, and the most bird-like experience is paragliding. Tighten your helmet's chin-strap, secure your harness, take a running leap, then you're gliding high in the air... Do look down!

(1)

Grindelwald
Switzerland

From a paraglider, your sense of perspective turns on its head: towns appear doll-like, forests that look forbidding on foot transform into fuzzy green carpets. In Grindelwald, you can experience this delightful disorientation in the midst of the rugged Bernese Alps: you'll soar above the north face of the Eiger (3967m/13,015ft), past triangular peaks that melt into evergreen forests and cow-dappled meadows. Grindelwald is popular with beginner paragliders: you can glide with an expert on a tandem flight.

Essential information: Grindelwald is an efficient 3hr by train from Zürich. Book ahead - it's immensely popular in both summer and winter.

Far left to right: Grindelwald, Switzerland; Queenstown, Lake Wakatipu and the Remarkables; tandem glide, Pokhara Valley

2

Queenstown
New Zealand

Queenstown is Australasia's adrenaline capital, and thrillseekers flock here to hike, heliski, ice-climb and more. Adventure-sports operators galore can take you into the pristine alpine scenery, which looks loveliest from the air: take flight from Coronet Peak to paraglide high above Lake Wakatipu and the snow-speckled Remarkables. And paragliding isn't the only way up. Queenstown offers skydiving, ziplining at Shotover Canyon, and precipitous bungy jumps like Nevis Bungy (134m/440ft).

Essential information:
You can paraglide year-round (weather permitting). Fly to Queenstown via Australia, or via Auckland International Airport.

3

Pokhara Valley
Nepal

Paragliding in the Himalaya places you at eye level with a true pantheon of giants. Valley wind currents will send you to lofty heights where you can admire conical Hiunchuli (6441m/21,132ft); Annapurna (8091m/25,545ft); and Machhapuchhre (6993m/22,943ft), a sacred peak that has never (legally) been climbed. After soaring with the vultures, land by the indigo expanse of Phewa Lake to come full circle with an inverted view of Machhapuchhre, reflected in the lake's glassy surface.

Essential information:
Flights launch from Sarangkot, 30min from Pokhara. Mid-mornings March-May and September-November have the best weather.

4

Marrakesh
Morocco

Deserts, villages and the epic Atlas Mountains: paragliding in Morocco shows you a panorama of different landscapes in a few short minutes. Take to the skies above Marrakesh to see golden sand dunes sculpted by the wind, desert plains awash in hazy sunshine and Berber villages scattered across the Kik Plateau. For those seeking a slow pace, Morocco also has hot-air balloon rides galore. For paragliders, top launch spots include Aguergour and Ait Ourir (respectively south and east of Marrakesh).

Essential information:
Spring and autumn have milder weather for leisure flights. Fly to Marrakesh from London, or take trains and a ferry from Algeciras.

"WATER DOES NOT RESIST
PLUNGE YOUR HAND INTO IT,
WATER IS NOT A SOLID WALL,
BUT WATER ALWAYS GOES
NOTHING IN THE END CAN
IS PATIENT. DRIPPING WATER
REMEMBER THAT, MY CHILD.
WATER. IF YOU CAN'T GO
GO AROUND IT.

WATER FLOWS. WHEN YOU
ALL YOU FEEL IS A CARESS.
IT WILL NOT STOP YOU.
WHERE IT WANTS TO GO, AND
STAND AGAINST IT. WATER
WEARS AWAY A STONE.
REMEMBER YOU ARE HALF
THROUGH AN OBSTACLE,
WATER DOES."

– MARGARET ATWOOD, *THE PENELOPIAD*

SKINNY DIPPING

Ahhhwhoomp... and you're under. Teeth clenched from the cold. Ahhhshhhure... you re-emerge from the water, laughing brightly, hairs on end. Skinny dipping is one of life's great freedoms: a spontaneous collision of giddy excitement and the right environment. Quick, there's no one around. Clothes off... and in! It doesn't matter if it's a swift dip in an Australian bay or a post-sauna plunge into a Finnish ice-hole, bathing *au naturel* dissolves self-consciousness. A bracing, bits-out splash-about swaps societal vulnerability for animalistic inhabitation – and the euphoric rush of fight-or-flight endorphins can leave you feeling reborn.

1

Jätkänkämppä
Finland
Up near the Arctic Circle, where huskies pant in the cold and the Northern Lights dance like psychedelic flames against inky-dark skies, there is a type of skinny dipping favoured by hardy Finns: *talviuinti* (ice-swimming). Lakes are frozen October to May, so locals carve out an *aavanto* (ice-hole) for the perfect post-sauna cool-off. At a bits-shrivelling -20°C/-4°F, even the quickest of sploshes sees skinny dippers reappear alive and bright-eyed.

Essential information:
Jätkänkämppä, a traditional *savusauna* (smoke sauna) in Kuopio, eastern Finland, is a great place to start.

2

Alexandra Bay
Australia
You won't need to pack your budgie smugglers for this glorious arc of pristine sand in Noosa National Park, some 120km (75 miles) north of Brisbane. It can all hang loosa at A-Bay, one of Australia's first and finest nudist beaches. Skinny dipping spots don't come much better, but only the most hardened of naturists make it to this remote east-coast shoreline. Most days, the only thing between your privates and Peru will be the South Pacific.

Essential information:
A-Bay is a 3km (2-mile) walk from Sunshine Beach; park at Seaview Terrace car park and head north to the signposted Coastal Walk and A-Bay.

3

Kurokawa Onsen
Japan
Volcanic-spring (onsen) bathing is among the most popular of Japan's ancient traditions – particularly with city dwellers, who repair to locations around the country for a revivifying dip, in the nude. Among the most picturesque are the springs of Kurokawa in the Kyushu prefecture, with over 30 baths: purchase a wooden *tegata* pass for access to three different onsen. Alcohol and tattoos (unless very small or covered in bandages) are verboten.

Essential information:
There are regular daily buses to Kurokawa Onsen from Aso (1hr), Kumamoto (2.5hr), Beppu (2.5hr) and Hakata Station (3hr).

4

Hague Lake
Cortes Island, Canada

It's a good ol' schlep up to Cortes from Vancouver Island, but you'll be glad to arrive: white-sand beaches, warm water (in summer); and a backdrop of the Coast Mountain Range's glacial peaks make this a spellbinder for skinny-dippers. And, the lake's no-motor rule and remote location ensures pristine swimming. Just watch out for kayakers! Back on land, hiking and biking await in the surrounding parks.

Essential information:
Ferries from Campbell River on Vancouver's northern side run to Cortes' Whaletown Terminal, an 18.5km (11.5-mile) drive from Hague Lake.

Clockwise, from top: lamplit Kurokawa Onsen, Japan; the way to the water on Cortes Island, Canada; relaxing after a post-sauna *aavanto* dip in Kuopio, Finland

TRIAL
BY FIRE

Find out where to test your taste buds' tolerance for extreme heat with this guide to the world's hottest chillies. But check the Scoville scale heat rating of each one first...

Pure capsaicin
16 million units

Carolina
Reaper chilli
2.2 million units

Trinidad Moruga Scorpion
Heat: Hotter than the gates of hell
Scoville heat units: 2 million
The evil-looking Trinidad Moruga Scorpion has a fearsome sting in its tail, despite being knocked off the top spot by the Carolina Reaper. Sample it as hot sauce in Trinidad and Tobago.

Carolina Reaper
Heat: Hotter than a thousand suns
Scoville heat units: 2.2 million
More than 400 times hotter than Tabasco sauce, the world's hottest chilli will reduce body-building construction workers to tears. Order seeds from South Carolina's PuckerButt Pepper Company and bring on the burn!

Pepper spray
2 million units

Naga Bhut
Jolokia chilli
1 million units

Habanero
Heat: Incendiary
Scoville heat units: 100,000–350,000
When Mexicans want to turn up the heat, they reach for the habanero, an innocent-looking bell-shaped pepper containing the culinary equivalent of molten lava. Habaneros add pep to the scorching salsa served on the side with most meals in Mexico's Yucatán peninsula.

Naga Bhut Jolokia
Heat: Napalm
Scoville heat units: 1 million
A key ingredient in Assamese curries, stir-fries and chutneys, Naga 'ghost chillis' are also smeared over fences as a deterrent to wild elephants. To sample at source, visit food stalls at rural *haat* (open-air markets) in the central hills of Assam, northeastern India.

Habanero chilli
350,000 units

Bird Eye chilli
100,000 units

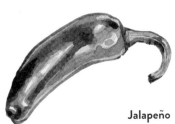

Jalapeño chilli
8000 units

Jalapeño
Heat: Inglenook fireplace
Scoville heat units: 2500–8000
The original 'hot' chilli, this moderate scorcher is still grown in vast quantities in the Veracruz and Chihuahua districts of Mexico. Chipotles (smoked jalapeño peppers) are a key ingredient in Mexico's legendary adobo sauce.

Bird Eye
Heat: Eye-watering
Scoville heat units: 50,000–100,000
Compared to the record-breaking Carolina Reaper, Thailand's bird eye chilli is as weak as a kitten – but try telling that to anyone who has numbed their tongue on *som tam*, a fiery Thai salad made from raw bird eye chillies, lime juice and green papaya.

Tabasco sauce
2500 units

TAKE A WATERFALL SHOWER

Don't just contemplate the view, take the plunge! Splashing alfresco beneath the spray of a real, rippling waterfall makes you feel that bit more revived and alive. Of course, you can't just jump into any old waterfall. That plummeting power can create dangerous currents, froth and tumult; and some plunge pools are full of gnarly rocks. But pick the right pool – perhaps a small stream-trickled mountain lake or a hidden gushing gorge (clothing optional) – and there's no finer nor more fun way to wash.

1

Hot Springs Waterfall Finca el Paraíso, Guatemala

A short hike leads down steps towards this natural spa: the sizzling thermal waters of the Rio Dulce (Sweet River) crash over a wall of rocks and into an ice-cool pool, cloaked in luscious jungle. Clamber with care over the rocks and slip in; witness up close the steam rising from the bath around you, or take a seat on the outskirts of one of the caves beneath the falls to enjoy an alfresco warm shower.

Essential information:
You can hop on a bus from Rio Dulce town to Finca el Paraíso. Expect to pay a small entrance fee.

Far left to right: Finca el Paraíso, Guatemala; Kerikeri's Rainbow Falls, New Zealand; Tat Kuang Si Falls, Laos

2

Lower Ddwli Falls
Brecon Beacons, Wales

More than 20 pools dot a 8km (5-mile) stretch of river in a leafy location known – unsurprisingly – as Waterfall Woods. Lower Ddwli Falls has an arcing cascade, where spray bounces off the nearby plantlife. A huge open pool has lots of swim space and, with luck, on fair-weathered days you can see plentiful rainbows. Spend the day sampling as many pools as you can, or plan to come back for more.

Essential information:
It will be chilly for most of the year, so come prepared with wetsuits, layers and a thermos.

3

Rainbow Falls
Kerikeri, New Zealand

Starting from Kerikeri Basin, track between kauri and totara trees, past Wharepuke Falls and the Fairy Pools, towards the tumbling sounds of the 27m-high (88ft) Rainbow Falls, or Waianiwaniwa (Waters of the Rainbow). Reaching this gorgeous gush, you'll notice how the single-drop tumbles over volcanic basalt into a perfect plunge pool. Even on dull days you can catch a rainbow glinting in the fall's spray.

Essential information:
The waterfall sits along the 10min-long Rainbow Falls Walk.

4

Tat Kuang Si Falls
Laos

These many-tiered falls, just 30km (19 miles) from Luang Prabang, tumble over limestone formations into a series of cool, swimmable pools. The alluring turquoise colouring is thanks to the limestone's high levels of light-reflecting calcium carbonate. You can jump, dive or swing off ropes into the pools, and a somewhat slippery jungle trail that sits alongside the falls leads you right up to the top of the cascades. The term 'Edenic' does not do it justice.

Essential information:
Consider visiting via a bike ride, but be prepared: there are two long, steady hill-climbs on the route.

EXPLORE
A LIBRARY

You don't have to travel far
to explore other places: your
local library is the gateway
to a world of stories and
new voices. And if it is as
spectacular as Trinity College's
library in Dublin (left), the
Stadtbibliothek in Stuttgart,
the State Library Victoria
in Melbourne or Baltimore's
George Peabody Library, then
lucky you.

TAKE AN URBAN HIKE

Nobody walks in LA – a statement so true it's been immortalised in song. But walking in a city can give you a taste of the whole that's impossible at driving speed. While away a few hours on the slow path, and see the familiar on foot. Carve your way into a quilt of individuated neighbourhoods and connector boulevards that link patchwork communities. Catch it while you can – the skyline may never look the same again.

1

Sydney
Australia

Australia's largest city has one of the world's most spectacular urban coastlines. And if you have a week to spare you can hike the entirety of its Great Coastal Walk – all 94km (58 miles) of it. The route begins at Barrenjoey, at the tip of Sydney's northern beaches, and trips a sandy course to Manly before heading inland to the Harbour Bridge and southern shores of Sydney Harbour. Pick up a shorter slice of it if you've less time, from Bondi to Coogee.

Essential information:
The Bondi to Coogee Coastal Walk is 6km (3.7 miles).

Far left to right: Midtown's Bryant Park, New York City; Dragon's Back Ridge on the Hong Kong Trail; Bondi to Coogee walk, Sydney

2

New York City
USA

Everyone walks in NYC, and trying to single out a route might be a challenge. Still, we suggest linking a few neighbourhoods in a self-guided tour at your own pace through the hustling masses. Start at Washington Square Park in Greenwich Village and walk up Fifth Avenue, north past Bryant Park and into Midtown. Moving into Uptown, skirt Central Park then continue to meander north through Marcus Garvey Park in Harlem, where that mythic street ends at the Harlem River.

Essential information:
In Manhattan, streets are numbered in ascending order, and avenues by east to west, with Fifth Avenue marking the east-west divide.

3

Berlin
Germany

Best known to cyclists, the Berlin Wall Trail follows the course of the infamous Wall that once divided West Berlin from East Germany. Seventeen years after it was famously breached (in 1989), the Wall was transformed into a 160km (99-mile) hiking and cycling path. The trail is signposted and has interpretative boards detailing the 28-year story of the Wall and of Germany's division, including memorials to those who tried to escape. The Berlin Wall Orientation System, located in the city centre, also features maps and listening stations.

Essential information:
The trail is split into 14 sections.

4

Hong Kong
China

The Hong Kong Trail snakes 50km (31 miles) around five country parks on Hong Kong Island, from Victoria Peak and its cracking views of Victoria Harbour to Tai Long Wan, a beautiful surf beach on the east coast. Take this route and you'll effectively be walking from the island's highest point to its lowest, via waterfalls, reservoirs and ruins. The S-shaped stretch of the Dragon's Back ridge is arguably the best section if you're limited on time.

Essential information:
The trail is divided into eight sections, some of which can be combined to turn the route into a three- or four-day hike.

TOTAL ECLIPSE

Nothing reminds us of the celestial ballet unfolding around us as watching an eclipse of the sun or moon. Here's when and where to see upcoming eclipses.

Total Solar Eclipses

When: 20 April 2023
Where: South and East Asia; Australia; Pacific Ocean; Indian Ocean; Antarctica

When: 8 April 2024
Where: Parts of western Europe; North America; Central America and the Caribbean; Pacific Ocean; Atlantic Ocean; Arctic

When: 12 August 2026
Where: Europe; North and East Asia; North and West Africa; most of North America; Pacific Ocean; Atlantic Ocean; Arctic

When: 2 August 2027
Where: South and West Europe; South and West Asia; most of Africa; East of North America; Atlantic Ocean; Indian Ocean

When: 22 July 2028
Where: Southern parts of South and Southeast Asia; Australia; Pacific Ocean; Indian Ocean; Antarctica

Total Lunar Eclipses

When: 13–14 March 2025
Where: Most of Europe, Asia, Australia and Africa; North America; South America; Pacific Ocean; Atlantic Ocean; Arctic; Antarctica

When: 7–8 September 2025
Where: Europe; Asia; Australia; Africa; western parts of North America; eastern parts of South America; Pacific Ocean; Atlantic Ocean; Indian Ocean; Arctic; Antarctica

When: 2–3 March 2026
Where: Eastern Europe; Asia; Australia; North America; most of South America; Pacific Ocean, Atlantic Ocean; Indian Ocean; Arctic; Antarctica

When: 31 December 2028–1 Jan 2029
Where: Europe; Asia; Australia; Africa; North and West North America; Pacific Ocean; Atlantic Ocean; Indian Ocean; Arctic

When: 25–26 June 2029
Where: South and West Europe; South and West Asia; Africa; most of North America; South America; Pacific Ocean; Atlantic Ocean; Indian Ocean; Antarctica

STARLIT CINEMA

Kick back at a theatre where the backdrop is as dramatic as the action on screen – choose your setting wisely and you can make it a movie to remember. In a world where we constantly view films on planes, phones and –all too often – alone, the communal act of movie-watching feels magical, especially when you're somewhere stunning: it quite literally gives you goosebumps. Cosy up under your blanket, sip on a chilled drink and savour freshly popped popcorn, ready for the action to begin.

1

Red Rocks Amphitheatre
Colorado, USA
At 2000m (6562ft) above sea level, the Red Rocks Amphitheatre sits in the shadow of two towering sandstone monoliths, providing both perfect acoustics and an awesome natural backdrop. Red Rock's history of arts is ancient – the Ute Tribe once used the space as a gathering place for music and dance. Completed in 1941 and seating almost 10,000 people, the amphitheatre hosts a number of events throughout the year, including screening a mix of '80s, '90s and 2000s cult-classic movies.

Essential information:
You can bring your own food in, but not booze. It can get chilly at night at this altitude: bring layers.

2

Sun Pictures
Broome, Australia
The world's oldest outdoor cinema, Sun Pictures is located in the Chinatown district of Broome, in remotest Western Australia. The tin-fronted building started life as an Asian-goods emporium, switching to showing silent movies in 1916. Now on the State Register of Heritage Places, it screens mainstream and indie movies that you can enjoy from comfy canvas chairs perched under the stars. And it'll even provide mosquito repellent if you forget your own.

Essential information:
BYO is not permitted. Snacks and drinks – including ice cream and homemade choc bombs – can be purchased at the kiosk.

3

The Galileo
Cape Town, South Africa
On Thursdays and Sundays from November to April each year, the super-lush croquet lawns of Kirstenbosch, Cape Town's oldest botanical garden, host cinephiles from all over the city. Set against the eastern slopes of Table Mountain, the open-air site favours classics and crowd-pleasers, paired with gourmet food trucks. The spot happens to be sheltered from the elements, so don't be put off by fiendish Cape Town winds.

Essential information:
You can bring your own alcohol and pack a picnic, but leave blankets and chairs at home. Arrive early to reserve a seat.

4

Cine Thisio
Athens, Greece

Since 1935, Athens' oldest outdoor theatre, the Cine Thisio, has been wooing tourists and locals alike. Family-run since 1980, it shows a mix of classics and new studio releases, and takes film selection very seriously. Rather than distract, the 5th-century-BCE Acropolis, topped by the iconic Parthenon, only enhances the experience, as do the old-school film projector, the neon art deco entrance and the rampant ivy that runs riot over everything except the seats and the screen.

Essential information: Cine Thisio screenings begin around late April/early May and end near late October.

Clockwise, from top: Broome's Sun Pictures, Australia; Colorado's Red Rocks Amphitheatre, USA; alfresco cinema essentials: popcorn and a blanket

"NOT JUST
THOUGH – THE
THE TREES IN THE
AND BREATHING.
WATCHING

BEAUTIFUL, STARS ARE LIKE FOREST, ALIVE AND THEY'RE ME."

– HARUKI MURAKAMI, *KAFKA ON THE SHORE*

COOK SOMETHING YOU CAUGHT

Foraging is the antithesis to the ready meal: no additives (except maybe some soil); 'packaging' courtesy of Mother Nature. Not only do you get a primal reconnection with the earth but a cave-person smugness in fending for yourself. Autumn is bonanza time as fruits ripen on trees, berries appear as morsels of sweet delight on bushes, and mushrooms sprout from the damp ground. In the seas and rivers mackerel and salmon are readily caught. Keep your eyes open and a basket at the ready.

1

Pluck berries
Sweden

Sweden is serious about foraging. It's even written in the nation's law: *allemansrätten* (every man's rights) grants permission to hike, camp and berry-pick on another's land, as long as it's done respectfully. A huge percentage of the country's berries is left unpicked each year, so head out into ample empty spaces in summer to find wild food – pick of the crops are sweet strawberries, golden cloudberries, blueberries and lingonberries.

Essential information:
There are easily accessible public transport options from major cities such as Stockholm to nearby forests and nature reserves.

Far left to right: lingonberries, Sweden; mushrooming amid fall colours in Fontainebleau, France; Nova Scotia scallops, Canada

2

Dive for scallops
Nova Scotia, Canada

Clinking masts, bright-painted huts, a salt-whiff on the breeze – the ocean defines Canada's easterly Nova Scotia province. Its Atlantic waters are a veritable fish soup and, equipped with a Recreational Scallop Licence, you can dive down and take a portion for yourself. The fishing limits are set at 50 a day – more than enough for a magnificent mollusc feast. Add a dash of soy sauce, and you can go ahead and eat them straight from the shell.

Essential information:
Scallop season runs from Easter to the end of July.

3

Pick wild garlic
UK

Between March and May, many British woodlands start to stink. Wild garlic – or ramsoms – grow rampant, their shiny green leaves and cheery white flowers cloaking many an undergrowth and infusing the air with anti-vampiric fumes. Boot up and hike off with a pair of scissors – the leaves are best snipped carefully at the stem, and more flavoursome before the plants begin to bloom.

Essential information:
The perfect picking season is late winter through to the end of spring.

4

Fungi foraging
France

In the great forests of eastern France, autumn's seasonal delicacy is the mushroom, which you'll see piled high in town markets. If picking your own as a novice, it's best to stick to a couple of varieties you can identify with certainty. Start with chanterelles, which are the colour and smell of apricots, and the bulbous cep. And don't be put off by the name of *trompettes de la mort* (trumpets of death) – these inky shrooms are non-poisonous and very tasty.

Essential information:
Mid-August to mid-September see the best crops.

SWIM WITH FISH

Forget the chlorine-y sameness of the pool and get wild with aquatic life. Sure, pools are great for swimming laps or cooling off during a scorching summer. But make it a life goal to swim with fish – or sea turtles, or rays, or sharks – in an ocean, lake or river. Unlike in pools, this swimming is full of surprises. You might spot a dolphin breaching. You might hear the crick-crack sound of a loggerhead snacking on coral. You might feel the tickle of minnows nibbling your toes. Wild!

1

Lady Elliott Island
Australia
Think 'Great Barrier Reef,' and many of us imagine scuba diving. But at Lady Elliot Island, the southernmost of the reef's coral cays, you don't need to go deep to see green sea turtles, manta rays, speckled carpetsharks and sherbet-coloured parrotfish. This eco-tourism destination is a snorkelling fairyland, with a family-friendly shallow lagoon on the eastern side, and a deeper coral garden to the west. From June to October, humpback whales migrate past, filling the water with eerie whale song.

Essential information:
The island has a small eco-resort; its airstrip has flights from several mainland Queensland cities.

2

Tulum
Mexico
On Mexico's Yucatán Peninsula, the area around Tulum is pocketed with cenotes, limestone sinkholes filled with groundwater. Many of these cenotes are popular swimming spots, with cave walls, vines and half-submerged rock formations serving as backdrops. Pick a few and go cenote-hopping: plunge into the vodka-clear water of the Jardín del Edén cenote and spy flitting crayon-coloured fish, or swim through the massive cave system of Gran Cenote alongside sea turtles. Afterwards, find a sunny rock and lounge with the iguanas.

Essential information:
There are several hundred cenotes in the Tulum area; ask around to find the most suitable for your needs.

3

Donsol
Philippines
Two things: first, whale sharks are sharks, not whales. Second, they are not the man-eating kind. So feel reassured when a ginormous spotted fish whooshes past as you float through the warm waters of Donsol Bay. From November through June, whale sharks, known in Tagalog as *butanding*, flock to the area, and visitors are permitted to swim and snorkel (though not dive) nearby. Be aware that they're on their own schedule – boat operators don't feed or lure the whale sharks, so sightings happen by luck only.

Essential information:
To get to Donsol, fly from Manila to Legazpi City, and then take a 2hr van trip.

4

Nassau
Bahamas

Mega-resort Atlantis on Nassau's Paradise Island is a world unto itself, with its very own 'ecosystem', Aquaventure, a 62-hectare (154-acre) waterscape of artificial reefs, lagoons and mega-tanks. Non-divers can don helmets with breathing tubes and stroll underwater through the shark habitat, coming snout-to-snout with reef and nurse sharks. No, it's not natural. But it IS fun. Bring a waterproof phone pouch to snap unforgettable pictures.

Essential information: Paradise Island is connected by causeway to downtown Nassau. The resort runs airport shuttles.

Clockwise, from top: swimming with whale sharks in Donsol, Philippines; snorkel with green turtles around Lady Elliott Island, Australia; Tulum cenote, Mexico

A CHANCE ENCOUNTER

Travis Levius welcomes serendipity in Chiang Mai.

I like to say I've always embraced the maxim 'live your life like it's a movie', but never imagined I'd live life *in* a movie. Impactful encounters with locals and travellers are the greatest strokes of luck I'd expect on any given journey, but during my first trip to Thailand, I encountered what I can literally say was a once-in-a-lifetime opportunity.

It all started with a – rather extravagant, as it happened – work trip. I (very happily) joined a luxury four-day press junket to Phuket, where the itinerary involved hopping on billionaire-grade superyachts and slumbering in beachside villas. As I said, rather extravagant. Since it was my first visit to the country, I decided to extend my stay as a solo traveller for a month to immerse myself in the surrounds, albeit on a slimmer personal budget. My set plans scarce, I opened myself to the freewheeling spontaneity of unplanned travel.

Around two or three days in, I received word from a Facebook group I'd recently joined that the director Spike Lee – of *BlacKkKlansman* fame – was coming to Chiang Mai. To shoot a Vietnam War movie called *Da 5 Bloods*. And he was looking for extras.

My initial thought: is this a sham?

Turns out, it was very, very real, but it also posed a real dilemma: should I cut my Phuket stay short and head to a new-to-me city within 48 hours and take a – very small – chance at starring in a Hollywood film...or minimise the risk of disappointment, and upheaval, by

staying put and playing it safe in paradise? I chose the former.

I flew into Chiang Mai, quickly refreshed myself at my modest Airbnb (where was the superyacht when I needed it?) and headed out the same evening. I arrived at a meet-and-greet casting session with the director. I filled in my casting details, got my picture taken and had a short but sweet encounter with the man himself. Lee and I both have Brooklyn ties – the last place I'd expect to shake hands with the film visionary was a thrumming city in northern Thailand, but I went with it.

Just days later an email arrived, announcing my placement as an extra for a day. But it was the email I received after this that would change my life.

Casting wanted me to be a stand-in for Chadwick Boseman. The late, great *Black Panther* star Chadwick Boseman.

Somebody pinch me!

At the time, I didn't even know what a stand-in was. (A body-double, of sorts, who helps a primary actor hit their marks with camera and lighting placement, if you're also wondering). Admittedly, I also didn't know who I was standing in for until I did some research.

Before I could register what was really happening, my no-frills solo trip had morphed into a two-month cinematic odyssey with some of Hollywood's most legendary players.

Filming *Da 5 Bloods* made me a morning person, if temporarily so. Requisite 4.30am call-times for transfers to any given set location in northern Thailand became an exciting guessing game: what natural beauty will be revealed once the sun's delicate glow has painted the landscape? One day it was an amphitheatre of green-carpeted limestone peaks in verdant Chiang Dao, where a plane prop anchors the scene of Black American soldiers exchanging gunfire with local forces. On another, streams from a plunging Mok Fa Waterfall

gurgle along Doi Suthep-Pui National Park's forest floor. All this while Lee directs me where to stand so that Boseman can hit his mark for key scenes.

These early mornings grew on me, being the most bearable periods of waking during the several 10- to 12-hour shooting days in intense spring climes. Multimillion-dollar film budgets do not shield one from temperatures that reach 35°C (95°F) by late morning. We spent our days head-to-toe in army get-up, sweating and swatting flying pests. On-location is no glittery walk in the park, but the experience was nonetheless one of epic proportions.

There is something to be said about leaving some wiggle room for wonderment. From someone who had a tendency to over-plan, I found such joy in surrendering to the whims of chance. Stumbling upon a – literal – blockbuster of an opportunity, and having the time and space to take it on, served as a reminder that life is often best lived unscripted.

JUMP FOR JOY

Just jumping can benefit your heart and lungs and build fitness but, as these false killer whales off La Paz in Baja California know, it's also a really healthy expression of joy. A playful attitude to life keeps us forever young and helps maintain good mental health.

LOOK UP!

Stand in Florence's Uffizi Gallery to have your mind blown by simply looking up once in a while. We spend most of our time at eye level, and a change of perspective opens up a new dimension of marvels: whether in the abstract patterns of a forest canopy or, of course, the urban canyons of cities like New York.

CLASSIC COCKTAILS

Taste is a shortcut to memory: don't just sip an iconic cocktail in the city that it was invented – try concocting the recipe from home for whenever you want to return.

SIDECAR
PARIS

The Method
1 part Cointreau
1 part lemon juice
2 parts cognac

Pour all the ingredients into a cocktail
shaker filled with ice. Shake well then
strain into a chilled cocktail glass.

The Tale
The Ritz Hotel in Paris, France claims
the Sidecar as its own creation, dreamed up
in the first decade or two of the 20th century.
But after a couple of these punchy numbers
it's no surprise that memories are hazy. The
French School advocates equal parts of
the ingredients; the English School
prefers a little extra depth.

NEGRONI
FLORENCE

The Method
1 part gin
1 part Martini Rosso
1 part Campari
orange peel for garnish

Combine all the ingredients in an ice-filled
glass. Add a twist of orange peel to garnish.

The Tale
The story goes that in 1919 Count Camillo
Negroni of Florence asked for a more
potent version of his favourite cocktail, the
Americano. The barman switched soda water
for gin and the lively little Negroni was born.
Florence remains the ideal place to
sample one as an aperitivo.

MOJITO
CUBA

The Method
1 part lime juice
2 parts white rum
1 teaspoon of sugar
mint leaves
soda water

Muddle the lime juice, sugar and mint leaves
in a glass. Fill the glass two-thirds full of ice
and add the rum. Top up with soda water.

The Tale
Ernest Hemingway would relieve the
heat of Cuba with this refreshingly minty
drink. It was a refinement of the mint-sugar-
rum-and-lime Drake cocktail, and was first
recorded in the 1930s.

SINGAPORE SLING
SINGAPORE

The Method
1 part gin
1 part cherry brandy
1 part Bénédictine
1 part fresh lime juice
2 parts soda water
1 dash Angostura bitters

Mix all the ingredients, except the soda water
and bitters, in an ice-filled glass. Stir in the
water, then add a splash of bitters.

The Tale
At the Long Bar in Raffles hotel,
Singapore, the Gin Sling was the perfect
antidote to the steamy climate; then a
barman added a dash of fruitiness to
invent the Singapore Sling.

FREEFALL

What compels a person to jump out of a perfectly serviceable aircraft and fall to Earth at 120mph (193kph)? Skydivers give conflicting answers: it's the adrenalin rush and the sense of peace; it's the freedom and the responsibility. Find out for yourself by making a jump; most nations have a parachuting association that accredits schools. Two of the most scenic scenes to descend over include the 4877m-deep (16,000ft) Fox Glacier in New Zealand – offering a petrifying one-minute-plus freefall – and Everest's drop from an altitude of 5486m (18,000ft).

TAKE A COLD-WATER PLUNGE

It's the electrifying, all-body inhale after plunging yourself into velvety, icy depths that seals the deal – cold water is as addictive as it is daunting. From invigorating dunks to restorative wild swimming, it's not just the numerous health benefits that make cold-water experiences so beguiling. There's a meditation in the process, in meeting yourself in the water as the initial shockwaves flow into endorphins – indeed, this is such a known adage that cold-water swimming devotees will probably have told you so, before you've even asked.

1

Copenhagen Harbour
Denmark

For chilly dips accompanied by a killer skyline view, Copenhagen is hard to beat, with a collection of harbour baths and bathing zones adorning its picturesque waterfront. Stretching from the buzzing Islands Brygge neighbourhood to chic Nordhavn, this collection of pools and platforms along the dazzlingly clear harbour are all open to the public, complete with springboard-studded diving pools to make taking the plunge all the more exhilarating. Head to a cosy café afterwards to keep the *hygge* going.

Essential information:
The harbour is served by a number of metro stations, but the easiest to head to for swimming spots are Islands Brygge and Nordhavn.

Far left to right: Dublin's Forty Foot from above; Kalvebod Bølge swimming platforms, Copenhagen; ice-swimming in Harbin, China

2

3

4

The Forty Foot
Ireland

A hearty faceful of the fresh, salty spray of the Forty Foot, at the tip of Sandycove's Dublin Bay, is all you'll need to be enticed into the iconic waters of this rugged promontory. A men-only swim spot until 1974, dedicated locals and cold-water pilgrims alike adorn this speck of coastline year-round to sample its renowned charms. The traditional Christmas Day swim has an added atmosphere of festivity and community that'll truly warm the heart – if not the extremities.

Essential information:
Forty Foot is a short train
ride from Dublin city
centre, a 20min walk from
Dun Laoghaire or a 5min
walk from Dalkey.

Ice-hole swimming
Finland

This is a tradition that's been hundreds of years in the making, so it's nigh on impossible to visit any Finnish town or city in the colder months and not sample ice-hole swimming. It's as simple as it sounds, requiring nothing more than a hole carved in a frozen lake, so those so inclined can slither on in for a quick submersion. Most public ice-swimming holes in cities and larger towns are pre-cut, and more often than not, accompanied by a highly enticing sauna.

Essential information:
In any Finnish town or
city, simply ask a local
about where to find the
nearest *avanto* (ice-hole).

Harbin's Songhua River
China

Where better for a cold-water flex than the 'ice city of China' itself? Harbin is so-called because of its world-famous Ice and Snow Sculpture Festival (held January to March), and the city's Songhua River is great for a bracing dip in the winter as it freezes over and becomes the site of various ice sports – including swimming. If you're feeling a little apprehensive, you can just look on as hardy locals put hairs on their chests with a few lengths in the river's icy depths.

Essential information:
Songhua River near Harbin
Road Bridge is accessible
from the local train
station via a number of
local buses.

"I AM

SOFT
TO OFFER
TOUGH
TO DROWN

WATER

ENOUGH
LIFE
ENOUGH
T AWAY"

– RUPI KAUR, 'MILK AND HONEY'

SKYWALK

Walk above the clouds on the latest lofty lookouts. The Grand Canyon Skywalk was one of the first to allow visitors to walk on a glass platform cantilevered over the cliffside. In Alberta, Canada, the Glacier Skywalk at Jasper National Park has views over the Columbia Icefield. Or you could step into the void on Mont Blanc's Aiguille du Midi. Finally, the Aurland Lookout perches above Sognefjord in western Norway.

CHAPTER 2

A DAY

CREATE ART

In a day, or several, you can take a course in something creative, such as learning to make woodblock prints in Kyoto, Japan. And if that develops into a passion, great, but if not there's always another artistic endeavour to try elsewhere.

LOST & FOUND
AT CARNIVAL

Climb into a destination's skin at Carnival. Leave your inhibitions behind you and spend a day learning how to really let your hair down. Dance. Cheer. Find friends, then lose them again. Surrender to the insistent rhythm of brass bands, drumming processions and oversized headdresses. You are lost. Embrace it. Embrace someone. Most people will be: arms and shoulders intertwined, jumping, dancing in genuine party spirit.

1

Olinda Carnival
Brazil

To get the most out of Brazil's Carnival, you shouldn't so much go with the flow as completely give in to it. Unlike Carnival in Rio, in Olinda there are no spectators or ticket blockades: samba dancers, processions, musicians, Carnival-goers and giant papier-mâché puppets all funnel through the town's narrow cobbled streets. Get drawn into the soul emanating from brass bands led by beaten-up trombones and tarnished trumpets. Clap along to a high-speed military two-step-cum-polka, or lose yourself in the beats of a *maracatu* drum procession.

Essential information:
Olinda Carnival runs over a few days during February or March.

2

Junkanoo
Bahamas

This Bahamian Carnival / Mardi Gras hybrid, said to date back to pre-enslavement West African secret societies, sees the nation's streets filled with partygoers dressed in rainbow costumes and headdresses as impressive as towering birds of paradise. Once Midnight Mass is finished, off roll the floats: musicians drive the crowd wild with drums, cowbells, conch-shell horns and whistles. The floats, powered by individuals and weighing up to 90kg (200lb), vie for prizes and star in parades through the capital, Nassau.

Essential information:
Join in with the festivities between 26 December and 1 January.

3

Ati-Atihan
Philippines

This Christo-pagan beaded bacchanal, known to all as 'the mother of all Philippines festivals', is held on Kalibo, an island in a beach-fringed archipelago that's only an hour by plane from Manila. Expect dance, painted faces, parades and fabulous costumes honouring the traditions of the island's Indigenous people, all in celebration of Santo Niño (Infant Jesus). On the last day, a hand-held torchlit procession blazes the night sky en route to Kalibo Cathedral for a final prayer.

Essential information:
Ati-Atihan is held each January; the festival's biggest celebration usually falls on the third Sunday of the month.

4

Bon Om Touk
Cambodia

When the Tonle Sap River sees an extraordinary phenomenon, making an about-turn and flowing in reverse, it signals party season for Cambodia. Honouring this annual hydro happening, which coincides with an auspicious Buddhist full moon and is held in celebration of the victory of King Jayavarman VII over the Chams, are three days of fireworks, feasting and dragon-boat racing. The wildest celebrations are seen along Phnom Penh's Sisowath Quay and at the riverside parties thrown in Siem Reap.

Essential information:
The celebrations usually take place during October or November.

Far left to right: Carnival puppets on parade at Olinda; musicians jamming at Junkanoo; racing dragon-boats at Bom Om Touk

SLEEP IN A CASTLE

Oh, what a night! Play out all your palace fantasies and lay your head on the pillows of kings and queens of yore. Myriad luminaries have walked within the thick walls of European castle complexes – and so can you. Sleep in a plush four-poster bed, in a room full of exposed stone walls and a profusion of drapery. You'll feel like a fleeting part of the castle's story, more so than if you'd just made a day trip.

1

Dalhousie Castle
Midlothian, Scotland

You are sleeping in a place where Robert the Bruce; Mary, Queen of Scots; Oliver Cromwell; Sir Walter Scott; even Queen Victoria have spent the night. The 13th-century ancestral home of the Ramsay family became a hotel in 1972, but it still echoes with its illustrious past. There's a fire roaring in the drawing room, a restaurant in the dungeon and a spa in the old storage vaults. Pose by suits of armour, watch falcons fly across the grounds and listen for a piper striking up Robbie Burns' *Address to a Haggis*.

Essential information: Dalhousie is located just 13km (8 miles) from the capital, Edinburgh.

Far left to right: Dalhousie Castle, Scotland; Germany's Castle Hotel, Schönburg; one-of-a-kind bedroom at Château de Tennessus, France

2

Castle Hotel
Schönburg, Germany

Teetering on a hilltop beside the Rhine, parts of this bastion date back to the 10th century. It's as romantic as they come: the sumptuous rooms are bursting with character – number 22 has a particularly brilliant balcony – and are richly furnished with antiques and chandeliers; some have four-poster beds and open fireplaces. Electric carts whisk you and your luggage up from the car park below the castle's lofty perch.

Essential information:
The gastronomic restaurant is also open to non-guests by reservation.

3

Ashford Castle
County Mayo, Ireland

This regal estate is frequently voted one of Ireland's best hotels. As well as wow factor it offers ample lordly activities, from falconry and fishing to horse riding and clay-pigeon shooting. Built in 1228 as the seat of the de Burgo family, the castle's owners have included Arthur Guinness (of stout fame), who turned it into today's hunting and fishing lodge. The vast parklands hold forests, streams and a golf course.

Essential information:
The only way to see Ashford's restored interior is to stay or dine here, but the surrounding estate is open to the public.

4

Château de Tennessus
Poitou, France

The 600-year-old medieval, moated Tennessus is château perfection. Its upscale B&B has original spiral staircases, arrow slits, hoardings and a working drawbridge. The three uniquely decorated rooms each occupy a single floor, and are adorned in 14th-century-style handcrafted pieces and authentic wall hangings. Breakfast is served by candlelight in a stone chamber complete with original flagstone flooring and torches. In your downtime, row the moat, fish or amble in the period gardens.

Essential information:
Tennessus is just over 1hr from the city of Nantes in western France.

CHUCK OUT THE CHECKLIST

Sarah Barell doesn't follow an itinerary in Bali

Some places you pass through, others have an extra gravitational pull. Go for a week, end up staying for months. Or at least that is how it should be. But in a world where we increasingly travel with timetables and checklists, the art of allowing ourselves to be seduced by somewhere, letting a destination derail us – and our schedules – is being lost.

And more's the pity, as these magnetic planetary spots are, often, the last places you imagined you'd end up pausing. And thus the world surprises you, as it should. Take Bali. It's heaving with tourists, tainted with the scars of religious extremism and suffering from a rebranding by way of the blockbuster *Eat, Pray, Love*. But... there's a reason that this mystical Indonesian island became the 'pray' part of the story. There really is something so soul-stilling about its orderly tiers of rice fields, temple-like mountains and brilliant-white, jungle-fringed beaches.

Do as artists and travellers have done for a century: arrive for those beaches and stay for the grace of the island's interior. The central town of Ubud has been drawing creative types since the 1930s, seducing Europeans with spiritual, decorative and figurative painting, intricate batik and sculpture. In the face of mass tourism, Bali has somehow preserved its rich Hindu culture with dignity and smiles. Temples rise over the crashing ocean like serene gods; handmade offerings line the street corners – more colourful, even, than the island's myriad endemic butterflies and sudden, technicolour sunsets.

Bali is the place to master the art of doing nothing, to spend a while in gentle meditation and mindless contemplation. For travellers who let themselves simply 'be', Bali induces a case of eat, love, stay.

"THE IMPATIENT 'GIVE ME A PLACE SHALL MOVE THE PLACE DOES NOT TO STAND ON THE GO WITH HER

IDEALIST SAYS:
TO STAND AND I
EARTH.' BUT SUCH A
EXIST. WE ALL HAVE
ARTH ITSELF AND
AT HER PACE."

– CHINUA ACHEBE, *NO LONGER AT EASE*

FACE FEAR

Grab it! That thing you fear the most – grab it by the horns and crush it. Board a plane, settle into a saddle or step up onto that stage. Learn how to take pleasure in that thing your body has associated with anxiety, once you've tamed its power over you. There's nothing more exhilarating. First comes panic. Then comes adrenaline. Then comes the ease that you weren't expecting. This is pure exposure: there's no greater way to conquer a fear than to face it head-on.

1

Horseback safari
South Africa
Being taught to ride by a horse-whispering rancher is the best way to overcome equine nervousness. Triple B is a working ranch in the Waterberg Mountains, South Africa's borderlands with Botswana. A wilderness once beloved of Mandela, it's home to big game, bigger mountain ranges and hardy herds of Anglo-Arabs, Thoroughbreds and Boerperds. Activities include yoga-in-the-saddle and game viewing. There's nothing like catching up with a herd of giraffe to make you forget about your rising trot.

Essential information:
Stay at simple but upscale Horizon Lodge, based at Triple B Ranch.

2

A head for heights
Italy
Head to the peaks, pinnacles and rock towers of Italy's eastern Dolomites – since the 15th century, when French army captain Antoine de Ville scaled the peak of Mont Aiguille with a ladder, climbers have been mad about this corner of the Alps. Follow in the footsteps of WWI soldiers via the Vie Ferrate (Iron Ways), a skyscraping series of mountainside cables, metal rungs, rope ladders and chain bridges that allow access to some of Europe's most heart-stopping views.

Essential information:
Always check the weather in advance: 'easy' routes can become difficult when there is snow, ice, fog or rain.

3

Public speaking
Netherlands
One of the world's leading improv groups, Amsterdam-based Boom Chicago are responsible for helping launch the careers of Seth Meyers, Jason Sudeikis and Jordan Peele. The American troupe perform English-language stand-up and burlesque performances, and run classes and workshops in which you can master acting techniques that will transform your public-speaking presence. Learn about body language, breaking down the wall between speaker and audience, and refine that awe-inspiring finale.

Essential information:
Boom Chicago's performances take place in Amsterdam's Rozentheater.

4

Fear of flying

Many large airlines and private companies host courses designed to help aviophobes bring down their fear of taking flight. Most introductory flying lessons include a 'walk-around', where the pilot explains the basics of the instruments, plus the chance to take off, cruise and sometimes land a dual-control plane. Other courses use relaxation techniques and Cognitive Behavioural Therapy to aid neutralising the fear of take-off, turbulence and everything in between.

Essential information:
Consider Virgin Atlantic's
'Flying Without Fear'
course or the SOAR 'Conquer
Fear of Flying' programme.

From top: traverse Italy's Dolomites via Vie Ferrate; conquer fear of flying with an all-areas aeroplane tour

RECHARGE AT A WELLNESS SPA

Kamala Thiagarajan practises the art of Ayurveda in Kerala.

I booked my spa retreat the day I opened my refrigerator and found my reading glasses inside, propped up against a jar of olives and vying for space with a bunch of chocolate impersonating peanuts. You don't really need a break until you find something super-weird in there – like your neighbour's cat, or your favourite houseplant, a friend of mine texts. But I was done staring at screens.

Reporting the news often means obsessive, round-the-clock reading. In the process, you soak in blue light from a gazillion devices that effectively zap the melatonin from your cells, the very hormone that usually lulls other mortals to sleep. I'd worked non-stop for months, and my eyes felt like they could use a pair of toothpicks to prop themselves open.

And so, I find myself at the Taj Malabar Resort & Spa, situated in Willingdon Island in Kochi, the heartbeat of India's Ayurvedic wellness scene in Kerala. Surrounded by acres of natural scrub-jungle and marshes, the resort is set against the Arabian Sea. Many are surprised to learn that Willingdon Island is man-made, and part of the teeming city of Kochi. In this area, known as the Malabar, a roaring trade in spices, silks and other goods began as far back as the 14th century, just after a huge flood carved out this natural harbour in 1341.

I am seated in a small office, consulting with an Ayurvedic doctor. The view from the bay windows takes in schooners and sailboats lined up against the backdrop of billowy clouds, the sky slightly overcast. A cool breeze wafts through the air.

'My eyes feel like wedges of sandpaper,' I say (in my best whiny voice) as I sip on a welcome drink – a concoction of tangy lemon and tulsi (a herb from the basil family), with a dash of honey. 'They're dry, but they're also constantly watering.'

The doctor looks at me appraisingly for a minute. 'You have a *vata dosha*,' he says, referring to an individual's predominant disposition, which Ayurveda believes can cause problems when it goes out of whack. 'You are creative, energetic, also an insomniac and prone to dry skin. You will benefit from learning the healing ways of water and combining it with the principles of rest.'

It turns out that all I need is a massage and a bath.

In the modern world, a bath is functional – we're out before we're wet around the ears, the suds barely dry. In Ayurveda, the act of bathing is sacred, therapeutic and deeply nourishing – a healing experience that restores physical energy even as it removes accumulated toxins, sweat, grime and dirt.

Ayurvedic baths don't begin with water – they tend to end with it. Leading up to the process, however, are other therapies designed to soothe, relax and put you in a pre-meditative state. And so, my spa day begins with the Pada Mardana. My feet are immersed in a foot bath, the water laced with essential oils, and rose and jasmine petals that shimmer like starry sprinkles. The massage that follows stimulates the reflex zones of the feet, inducing a deep relaxation. I am then led to a steam bath. When I emerge, my skin feels soft and dewy.

Next comes an hour of Vishram, the part where I must learn to rest. I lie down on a massage table made of fine, walnut-coloured waga wood, soft and smooth as though polished over centuries of gentle care. And yet it is firm enough to support my aching back. As I glide into its warm embrace, I am acutely aware of how sharpened my senses are, even when I close my gritty eyes.

The therapist pours a thick, golden oil onto my back. This is Brahmi oil, an extract from the *Bacopa monnieri*, a tropical herb that is believed to enhance the memory (no more refrigerator escapades, I feel like texting my friend).

It acts as a mild sedative and relaxes tired muscles, my therapist tells me. 'We hold a lot of tension in our shoulders,' she says. Maybe more in the palm of our hands, I think. For the modern-day Atlas, the weight of the world has shrunk to the size of a cell phone.

The oil massage is followed up by the Sukha, a deep nourishing scrub, followed by herbal wraps, interspersed with warm towels that take over every inch of my skin, improving circulation. And lastly, I sit back in a bath. I've never felt so vibrant and, yet, so deeply sated. I can finally open my eyes without the waterworks.

I can see why the spa is named Jiva (meaning 'life') – it's a promise to help you get back in touch with your vital inner force, a way of breaking away from routine and re-connecting to the very core of your being.

'I need to rest more often,' I gush-text my friend.

'Sure,' she texts back. 'But you know why even trees find it so hard to stay away from social media? Because they're always logging in!'

I know where I'll be heading the next time I need to log out.

EXPLORE UNINHABITED ISLANDS

Carried ashore by whispering waves, the kayak skids to a stop on the sand. You're here. It's silent. This is it, paradise: an island of your own. With nearly eight billion people on this spinning ball, few can disconnect like this. No phone, no cars, no rush. Earth has an estimated two million uninhabited islands, from craggy out-in-the-elements skerries to shimmering atolls surrounded by water so clear it could anoint future saints. Exploring one reconnects travellers with nature's natural rhythms and shows us what life could be again.

1

Skellig Michael
Ireland

This shard of wrinkled red sandstone and aged grey slate shoots out of the Atlantic like an iceberg. Rough and raw, the island has remained uninhabited since it was abandoned by the holy followers of St Fionan some 700 years ago. A craggy staircase is cut into the rocks, leading to oratories and beehive cells, but Skellig Michael's chief appeal is its harsh, mist-covered, gale-blown conditions: an end-of-the-Earth meeting between you, Mother Nature and God.

Essential information:
Visitor numbers are limited on the Skelligs: book ahead. Boats depart from Ballinskelligs, Caherdaniel and Portmagee (May-Sep).

Far left to right: a clear day at Skellig Michael, Ireland; find castaway bliss at one of Panama's 365 San Blas Islands

2

San Blas Islands
Panama

Sleepy days on starfish-studded white beaches define the San Blas experience. The local Guna population runs the show here, and their hospitality is blissfully simple: just kick back in a hammock and gawp at the turquoise waters and bright-blue heavens. Only 49 of the 365 cays are inhabited, leaving plenty of people-free paradises to pick from. Hire a kayak and point towards the best-looking palm-topped atoll.

Essential information:
It's a 2.5hr drive north from Panama City to Carti, from where boats and water taxis head out to the San Blas islands.

3

Rubondo Island
Tanzania

Floating in Lake Victoria like a land that humans missed, Rubondo is Africa's largest island national park. Home to yawning hippos and darting bushbuck antelope, the island marries Tanzanian tranquillity with untouched beauty. Forested with palms, tamarinds and sycamore figs, it also has stunning lakeside beaches. Camp overnight and your only neighbours will be chimpanzees, elephants and giraffes.

Essential information:
Boats to Rubondo take around 30min from Kasenda, which is 6km (4 miles) to the north of Muganza on Lake Victoria.

4

Wayag Island
Indonesia

Like bright-green mushrooms sprouting from neon seas, Wayag's collection of karst atolls seem a vision from a psychedelic dream. Day-boats drop you on sandy slips that put Leo Di Caprio's beach to shame, and there are guided climbs for capable hikers. Some say the best of Wayag is underwater, though: dive or snorkel to see corals in full health, wobbegong sharks, and even the occasional manta ray.

Essential information:
Naturally you'll need a boat to get here, but you can hire a speedboat for a day-long round-trip from Waisai on the island of Waigeo.

THE MEAL OF A LIFETIME

You know it's slightly bonkers to spend a month's salary on a single lunch. But then you somehow manage to finagle a table at one of the world's best restaurants – and you don't think twice. The afternoon unfolds slowly, with course after course brought out and explained. You can ask the staff exactly how the juniper foam got that texture, and they know. You are surprised and delighted by this first-class culinary journey: your mission of experiencing pure pleasure is complete.

1

El Celler de Can Roca
Girona, Spain
This three-star Michelin restaurant unseated Noma as number one on influential *Restaurant* magazine's definitive list. The Roca brothers (Joan, Jordi and Josep) deliver on their respective areas of expertise – cuisine, wine cellar (consisting of tens of thousands of bottles) and desserts – and as a rule one of them is usually in the kitchen at any given time. Expect authentic Girona culinary masterpieces that combine 'countryside and science'.

Essential information:
Opt for the Feast Menu and you'll get about 15 named courses; the classic tasting menu serves seven courses.

2

D.O.M.
São Paulo, Brazil
D.O.M., meaning, 'to the greatest and best god', is rock-star chef Alex Atala's two-Michelin-star palace of gastronomy in downtown São Paolo. He and his team skilfully deploy modernist cooking techniques on traditional Brazilian ingredients, including indigenous Amazon produce like açaí, black rice and *pupunha* fruit sourced from regional farms and riverside communities. As Atala says, 'It is necessary to cook and eat like a citizen.'

Essential information:
The restaurant is open for lunch and dinner Monday to Friday, and for dinner only on Saturdays.

3

Alinea
Chicago, USA
Wünderkind Grant Achatz pushes theatrical boundaries with his 18-course 'molecular gastronomy' tasting menus – a recent example had dessert listed simply as 'balloon: helium, green apple'. Main-course dishes may emanate from a centrifuge or be pressed into a capsule; à la duck served with a 'pillow of lavender air'. Most exclusive of all, the private kitchen table experience seats parties of six. Vegetarians and vegans can be catered for with advance notice.

Essential information:
Note that there's no sign on the restaurant's door, just a number; it's at 1723 North Halsted St.

4

BRAE
Victoria, Australia

Sustainable, seasonal and undeniably adventurous food is served at this restaurant on chef Dan Hunter's idyllic homestead on the edge of the Otways, west of Melbourne. Much of the produce is growing around you, from the chooks and the vegetable garden to the orchards and the parcel of wheat sown exclusively for the home-baked bread. A walk after the three-hour meal underscores the relationship between land and food.

Essential information:
It's around a 2hr drive from Melbourne to 4285 Cape Otway Rd. You can stay overnight or explore the beautiful area.

Clockwise, from top: Brae's cottage and garden; perfect presentation and a tasting spread at Alex Atala's two-Michelin-starred D.O.M. in São Paulo, Brazil

FEEL THE PULSE OF AN INNER-CITY FESTIVAL

Nothing beats the arms-in-the-air, electric euphoria of a live-music festival, as the sun sets on a day of unbridled thrills. Add an iconic city skyline into the mix, however, and you've got yourself an elevated atmosphere that's hard to beat. Plus, let's face it, a much easier journey home. Inner-city festivals perfectly concentrate the beloved festival experience into exhilarating single shots, offering not only the chance to see global acts in more intimate settings, but local showcases and quirky activities in urban surrounds.

1

Le Guess Who
Utrecht, Netherlands

An explosion of diverse sounds from global artists, Le Guess Who focuses on blurring musical boundaries and platforming underrepresented talent. For a long weekend in autumn, the festival takes over the edgy Dutch city of Utrecht, filling pop-up venues, theatres, churches, warehouses and clubs with a unique blend of sounds. From humble beginnings, this genre-bending event is now attracting media attention and international renown.

Essential information:
Le Guess Who usually takes place in November, and runs for three to four days. Day passes are from €58.

Far left to right: Utrecht's Le Guess Who platforms upcoming acts like Pa Salieu and Alabaster DePlume; Barcelona's Primavera Sound, now staged in Buenos Aires

2

The Great Escape
Brighton, UK

Known as the UK south coast city's version of SXSW, The Great Escape prides itself on bringing fresh new talent and underground acts into the spotlight for one heady weekend of incredible music and the uninhibited fun. Scattering sets and performances across quirky pubs, bars and clubs, this exuberant festival is a great showcase of emerging artists, all against the backdrop of the UK's capital of good vibes.

Essential information:
The Great Escape usually takes place in spring, and runs for three to four days. Tickets start at £70.

3

Primavera Sound
Buenos Aires, Argentina

Made famous by its Spanish counterpart, this renowned festival draws the biggest names in music to some of the planet's most vivacious cities: Barcelona, LA, São Paulo, Santiago and, of course, Argentina's capital. Charging through Buenos Aires' venues and parks, the month-long event brings together globally recognised acts with smaller, grassroots shows and activities that keep the capital buzzing throughout.

Essential information:
Primavera Sound Buenos Aires usually takes place over four weeks between October and November. Day passes are around £80-100.

4

Rolling Loud
New York, USA

Where better to immerse yourself in glorious live hip-hop than the city that birthed the genre? Although hip-hop's conception is actually credited to the adjacent neighbourhood of The Bronx, Queens rises to the challenge by platforming the most sought-after artists in the game, from chart-topping headliners to underground acts. This celebration of New York's famed lyrical flows converges in the Citi Field parking lot.

Essential information:
Rolling Loud NY usually takes place over three days in September, at the Citi Field baseball stadium. Tickets from $230.

BY THE LIGHT OF THE MOON

There's something magical about moonlight. The way it bathes everything in a deep, silvery glow, looms large then high and lights up the sky so brightly even the stars retreat. If you're craving an altered perspective, eschew the sun and turn your day upside down. Seeing the world by the light of the moon offers a renewed sense of serenity and excitement, filled with promise and joy.

1

Hike

Sandstone Peak in California's Santa Monica Mountains, USA, makes for a perfect night-hike. You may glimpse an owl peering from the treetops, and grazing deer tracking down a midnight snack. The trail is clear enough to follow through the sagebrush and emerges onto a moonscape plateau between two peaks. The tallest is your goal, Sandstone, overlooking the Pacific Ocean, the water white-gold with the moon's reflections. Find a flat rock and take in the scene.

Essential information:
Starting at around 11pm means the moonglow should be bright enough to reveal the countryside's secrets.

2

Paddle

Paddling takes on a sloshing, calming quiet in the moonlight. Full-moon whitewater is commonly offered on Class II and III river runs, which supercharges the serenity with a safe shot of adrenaline. If it's the ocean for you, know that tides can get wicked during full moons, so check the tidal tables and ask local experts. But there's nothing more spectacular than stroking toward the golden patches of a melting moon.

Essential information:
In the USA, several outfitters host moonlight whitewater trips along the Lehigh and Delaware rivers in Pennsylvania's Pocono Mountains.

3

Run

Global urban trendsetters gather in large packs to take on runs through the night-time streets of the world's mega cities. You get to dodge the hottest part of day and exercise in spaces gloriously empty of their daily traffic. In New York, the Midnight Run sees participants race off in Central Park at the stroke of midnight on New Year's Eve, and in London athletic werewolves take part in Chase the Moon races, staged at the hallowed site of the 2012 Olympics.

Essential information:
The Midnight run is at 6.4km (4 miles), and Chase the Moon events vary between 5km (3 miles) and 10km (6km) races.

4

Cycle

Whether you're biking solo on a beach path, heading into town with pals for a night out or taking part in a community night-ride, moonlit cycles bring cool breezes, a real sense of freedom and a whole new way to see the landscape. Take part in Critical Mass in London, England; at Missouri's Moonlight Ramble, USA – claiming to be the world's original night-time bike ride – thousands of cyclists take a leisurely ride in closed-off streets flooded by moonlight.

Essential information:
The Moonlight Ramble falls on a night in August that's nearest to the full moon. Critical Mass is monthly.

Clockwise, from top: a moonrise kayak trip; keep eyes peeled for owls on the Sandstone Peak hike, California; enjoy people-free pathways on a moonlit cycle ride

MAKE A MUSICAL PILGRIMAGE

Johnny Cash, Howlin' Wolf, Elvis Presley: they all recorded classic albums at Sun Studio in Memphis, Tennessee. Visiting recording studios like this one and Chess in Chicago, Motown in Detroit and Abbey Road in London, is an unforgettable way of connecting with shared cultural history.

BACK TO NATURE

Trade travelling amidst civilisation for reconnecting with the wild. Guided nature walks or self-guided wildlife-watching are not only meditative but can reawaken senses dulled by city life. Find spectacular settings to witness nature's great annual rituals, from witnessing performing pink flamingos strutting their stuff to hearing the whooping mating calls of howler monkeys echo through the jungle. It's just as natural history writer Patrick Barkham says: such natural experiences are a sort of peaceful exhilaration.

1

Red deer
Scotland

On the islands of the Inner Hebrides off the west coast of Scotland, UK, magnificent red deer inhabit both the Isle of Jura and community-owned Isle of Rum. There are 900-odd red deer on Rum, most easily seen in the north around Kilmory, where they have been filmed for various nature shows. Stags stand at an impressive 1.3m (4ft) tall at the shoulder, with antlers that can be 1m (3ft) in length and have 16 points.

Essential information:
In addition to stag-rut-watching in October, Rum's rangers offer guided walks and wildlife-viewing - from butterflies to eagles.

Far left to right: spot red deer stags on Rum, Scotland; hear howler monkeys in Costa Rica's Parque Nacional Manuel Antonio; find flamingos in the Camargue, France

2

Howler monkeys
Costa Rica

Like deer, male howler monkeys are judged on the tenor and volume of their calls – and the forests of Parque Nacional Manuel Antonio on Costa Rica's west coast are a cacophony of whoops and barks. Featuring lush jungle, picture-perfect beaches and craggy headlands, this relatively small coastal reserve (680 hectares/1680 acres) brims with howlers. Hike its trails and enjoy views of the island-studded Pacific Ocean.

Essential information:
Beat the crowds and maximize wildlife sightings by buying tickets the afternoon before you visit and arriving early on the day.

3

Bower bird
Australia

The male satin bower bird furnishes his bower (an elaborate ground-based structure that acts as both a stage and a nest) with an assortment of blue and shiny objects, from flowers to bottle tops. Drop a flower of any other hue into his bower and he'll remove it in an instant. Find the colour-coordinated couples by bushwalking the 160km (100 miles) of trails in Queensland's 200-sq-km (77-sq-mile) Lamington National Park.

Essential information:
The bower birds' habitats include rainforest, shrublands and eucalyptus and acacia forest.

4

Flamingos
France

The marshlands of the Camargue in southern France are the setting for one of nature's most choreographed – and captivating – courtships. In rhythmic pink battalions, flamingos strut in their hundreds across the Pont de Gau ornithological reserve, which is perhaps the best place to see this performance. The reserve has 7km (4 miles) of trails, giving you every chance to see its avian inhabitants, and a care centre for sick and injured birds.

Essential information:
The park is open year-round from 9am until sundown. Some southern section trails are accessible to those with reduced mobility.

SEE A ONCE-IN-A-LIFETIME BLOOM

Witness a botanical miracle you'll never forget – a flower that only blooms every decade or century. We rely on flowers' predictability to mark seasons: poinsettias at Christmas, roses for Valentine's Day, tulips in spring. But there are flowers that buck the bonds of the human calendar, whose blooms can only be found once in a lifetime. Catching such displays combines the adventure of treasure hunting with the dedication of birdwatching. It's thrilling, but also bittersweet, knowing that the next time such a bloom appears on the Earth, you may be long gone. Is that not the very definition of YOLO?

1

Kinabalu National Park
Malaysia

The rafflesia looks less like a flower and more like the villain of a plant-themed video game. The enormous, rubbery bloom can grow to 120cm (47in) long, its five warty petals centred on a hole that appears to be filled with teeth. Oh, and it smells like rotting flesh... See this beast of a bloom in Malaysian Borneo's Kinabalu National Park. You'll need to take a tour to find a current blossom; the flower takes five years to grow and only blooms for a week.

Essential information:
The national park is about 2.5hr by bus from the Sabah state capital of Kota Kinabalu, which has an international airport.

2

Kerala
India

About every 12 years, the *Strobilanthes kunthiana*, known as the neelakurinji, turns the hills of Kerala a powdery pinkish-purple. Climb into the cool mountains of the Western Ghats, blanketed in tea and coffee plantations, where a small sanctuary protects these rare blooms, considered a symbol of love. One nomadic group calculates age by the number of blooms a person has seen, and honey from bees that feed on the flowers is especially prized.

Essential information:
The neelakurinji sanctuary is about 30km (19 miles) from the town of Munnar; book a 4wd tour.

3

Huascarán National Park
Peru

Though some 800 species of plant live in this mountain wilderness, the Queen of the Andes is rightfully the most iconic. The world's largest species of bromeliad, it can grow up to 15m (50ft) high. Its lifespan is the same as a human's – about 80 years – and in the wild it only blooms once. Hike the highland forest and glacial lakes of Huascarán National Park to spy the rare flower, which rather resembles an enormous ear of corn.

Essential information:
The bus from Lima to the park takes about 7hr; there's a closer airport at Trujillo.

4

Arizona
USA

Though it's called the century plant for its supposedly once-in-100-years blooms, this is a misnomer. The *Agave americana*, native to the Sonoran Desert, blooms once every 20 or 30 years, and its flower looks more like a tree, with bulbous, Dr Seussian yellow clusters. One place to catch it in bloom is the city of Tucson, home to several botanical gardens specializing in Sonoran plants, as well as numerous stunning hikes through the plant's territory.

Essential information:
Tucson is in southeast
Arizona; its closest major
airport is in Phoenix, 2hr
away by car or bus.

Clockwise, from top: neelakurinji bloom in Kerala; agave in Arizona; seek out the supersized (and smelly) rafflesia in Malaysian Borneo's Kinabalu National Park

STAY SOMEWHERE HAUNTED

Push your courage to its limit and spend the night in reputedly cursed lodgings. At Havana's Ambos Mundos hotel in Cuba, stay as near as you can to room 511, a former haunt of Hemingway's. Guests have claimed hearing his ghostly steps in the middle of the night; you can tour the still-intact room. Or spot the spectre of Marilyn Monroe in the corridors of the Hollywood Roosevelt Hotel in the heart of LA, where she's thought to be still enjoying the luxe life of suite 1200 where she lived for two years, eerily appearing to passers-by in mirrors throughout the hotel.

"WHEN YOU
IN YOUR HAND
LOOK AT IT,
WORLD FOR
I WANT TO GIVE
TO SOMEONE

TAKE A FLOWER AND REALLY IT'S YOUR THE MOMENT. THAT WORLD ELSE."

– GEORGIA O'KEEFFE

CAPTURING WILDLIFE

India Latham helps build bridges behind the camera in Yellowstone National Park.

It was another grey morning as I walked into the TV studio headquarters in London. My team and I gathered in the newsroom office. But, as ever, instead of dissecting the latest political scandal we were throwing out ideas for the latest travel show.

'A Yorkshire pudding museum is opening,' mumbled my colleague, eyebrows raised.

'It's Guinea Pig Appreciation Day next month,' contributed the intern.

It wasn't the most inspiring of ideas meetings I'd endured. Until my boss turned to me: 'We need somebody to make a show on the 150th anniversary of Yellowstone National Park.'

The name was familiar to me, but was one I'd never given much thought to. So, I did what I always do when I'm assigned a shoot, I nodded enthusiastically... then went away to Google it. Spectacular. Iconic. A world-leader in conservation. But what wasn't immediately clear from my search results was the dark history that had led to the park's inception. This was the challenge that lay ahead of me: to find a story that would fairly represent the contradicting nature of Yellowstone. It was my first half-hour documentary, something I'd been building up to in my career and a far cry from my usual films, often edited down beyond recognition: orange-throwing festivals, sheep cuddling and vegan butchers.

After calls to officious National Park Service staff and tourist board reps, I got through to Jason Baldes. Jason works with the Intertribal Buffalo Council, and down a crackly line he told me about the bison relocation programme. When Yellowstone was established, Native Americans who'd inhabited the area for 20,000 years prior were forcibly removed from the land. To eliminate their food source, frontier settlers killed off all the bison. The population of America's largest land mammal fell drastically from over 30 million to around only 200, and with those deaths disappeared the futures of many Native American tribes. Up until now, this history has remained largely untold in the park. But, thanks to a captive breeding programme, bison numbers in the park are now booming, and in an effort to return sovereignty to local Native American tribes, some of Yellowstone's oldest bison are being relocated back to tribal lands once more. Jason was one of the people responsible for this, and he invited me and the crew to visit.

'It's spiritual healing,' Jason said, 'putting away the atrocities, the problems that were imposed upon us. Restoring bison to our communities helps our cultural revitalisation. It heals the land, it heals us.'

Three flights later (budgets were slim), I arrived in Cody, Wyoming, the gateway to the world's first national park, with my presenter and assistant producer. I'd booked us into the oldest hotel in the town, a decision I deeply regretted as I lay there trying to sleep, bison heads mounted to the wall above my bed quietly judging me.

The next day we met for breakfast and nervously ran through the schedule. We were travelling out of season. The park service had desperately tried to persuade us to come later in the year but, as is often the case, the content was needed sooner rather than later. No amount of snowstorm warnings could delay us; we'd just have to make it work.

It didn't take long for us to find our first bison. As we approached the stately creature we slowed, winding down the windows. During my research I'd spoken to a wolf-tracker, who said: 'Yellowstone will throw at you whatever it feels like, you just have to stop and take it all in. That's the magic of it.' At the time I was mildly irritated at the vagueness of his advice, but now I understood. Moving with purpose, a herd of bison thundered past our car. As my assistant producer scrabbled for the camera I took a moment to take it all in. The sound of their hooves against the earth, the rancid smell of their matted coats, their humongous backs and disproportionately short legs, the dark pools of wisdom in their eyes. Suddenly it was clear to me why I was here: to learn from these animals, whose ancestors had inhabited this land long before we came along. That the cars all sat there with their engines turned off felt like a mark of respect.

As a documentary filmmaker I often find myself in the wildest of situations. Finding goats licking at my ankles, gliding through Lapland on a snowmobile in frigidly subzero weather, hanging off the top of a ship's mast. And in all these moments I've been staring down a lens trying to hold focus or making sure the sound is coming through OK. Remembering to stop and appreciate the moment is often a challenge, but I never lose sight of this platform that can amplify voices and tell stories that have, for whatever reason, remained untold.

'It's not just a Native American story,' Jason said, as a bald eagle flew over us. 'It's an American story.'

As I stood filming the bison slowly crowding around us, I realised more than ever the power that storytelling has to create change.

OPEN HOUSE

In any city, the urge to peek behind closed doors is almost overwhelming. Whether visitor or resident, there are places forbidden to all but a few: private houses, businesses, institutions. For the incurably curious, the Open House Worldwide movement offers some respite. On one weekend a year, in an increasing number of cities around the world (London, Dublin, Melbourne, Rome, New York and Chicago), many of those usually closed doors are opened to the public. Guided tours by architects offer a tantalising glimpse of a city's secret layers, such as London's Brutalist Trellick Tower, designed by Ernő Goldfinger.

SIGNATURE DISH

Emily Matchar gets cooking in Paris.

I was in Paris for the first time, and had received a gift to take a cooking class at the Ritz Escoffier School. My imagination was lit up like the Eiffel Tower at night. What would we be learning to cook? Pheasants in chestnut sauce? Foie gras soufflé? A cream-puff tower? Imagine my surprise, then, when I arrived in the Ritz's basement classroom and saw what we'd actually be making. Scrambled eggs. Yes, scrambled eggs – that cafeteria-chafing standard, that too-tired-to-cook weeknight standby. A monkey could make scrambled eggs. A chicken could make scrambled eggs.

But as the teacher in his tall white *toque* began to talk, a hush fell over the classroom and we all focused intently as his slim, elegant hands cracked eggs into a copper bowl. The secret to this simplest of dishes, he said, was to cook the eggs at a very low heat, stirring constantly with a fork in a gentle circular motion to keep the curds soft and delicate. As you stir, slowly add small lumps of butter and drizzles of cream. Most importantly of all, don't rush things.

Finally, he scooped tiny servings of the eggs into paper cups and passed them around the classroom for us to taste. They were – and this is really the only word to describe them – perfect. Like buttery, savoury, daffodil-yellow clouds.

Now, whenever I want to impress a guest or make a loved one feel special, I'll cook them 'my' signature scrambled eggs. Sometimes with chives. Sometimes mushrooms. Sometimes plain.

The lesson is this: there's value in perfecting a simple dish, whether a meticulously prepared cup of Chinese *pu-erh* tea, a flawlessly crispy grilled cheese sandwich, or a sublime bowl of spaghetti with olive oil and garlic. Perfect it. Make it yours. Then make it for everyone.

PADDLE THE STRESS AWAY

Is there anything more tempting than a stretch of glimmering, still water, waiting to be carved into by the bow of a kayak, canoe or board, and the flick of a paddle? Taking to the water is a mindful way to spend a day: whether solo or on a voyage with friends, there are multiple methods of propelling yourself through the planet's lakes, seas and rivers, feeling the spray on your face and exploring new surrounds. Kayaking around coves, paddleboarding a canal or canoeing between islands... whatever floats your boat, really.

1

Stand-up paddleboarding Norwegian fjords
It's hard to imagine more glassy, glistening waters to explore on a paddleboard than in the world-renowned fjords of Norway's west coast. There are numerous multi-day, guided SUP tours available, but with a little bit of research, setting sail on your own is SUPer straightforward: paddleboard rentals are dotted throughout the fjords' main tourist spots. And thanks to Norway's *allemannsretten* (every man's right), free camping along the way is always encouraged.

Essential information:
The district of Voss, not far from Bergen, is a good base for SUP exploration in the Fjords.

2

Sea kayaking Bay of Islands, NZ
New Zealand's Bay of Islands, as the name suggests, is a panoramic bay off the country's northern coast, bedazzled with lush islands and rugged islets. As such, it's a perennially popular destination for kayak exploration, with guided tours and private rentals both readily available. Even if you do set off alone, you're unlikely to stay that way for long, with schools of dolphins, pods of whales and seal colonies all regularly spotted in and around the islands.

Essential information:
Otehei Bay in Bay of Islands has a large kayaking centre from which you can rent equipment and book tours.

3

SUP yoga in Boulder Colorado, USA
In a city that has outdoor exploration pulsing through its veins, Boulder, Colorado – its expansive lakes and reservoirs, framed by the dramatically beautiful Rocky Mountains – is a great place to sample the gloriously mad mash-up of yoga and stand-up paddleboarding. For those with a strong core and a steady Drishti, this is a great way to feel at one with the water. (Those whose centre of gravity is a little more unstable might make a bit of a splash...)

Essential information:
Boulder Reservoir is home to the Rocky Mountain Paddleboard centre, which runs regular SUP yoga classes.

4

Portaging
Algonquin, Canada

A popular Canadian outdoor pursuit, portaging (carrying a watercraft over land) is an especially adventurous way of exploring beyond where water alone can take you. Ontario's Algonquin National Park is a portaging playground, with endless lakes, river networks and intriguing islands to discover. Recruit a few of your hardiest friends, rent a canoe and head off into the wilderness – what could be better?

Essential information:
The national park has numerous canoe rental facilities throughout, as well as a portage store.

Clockwise, from top: plot a portaging path through Ontario's Algonquin National Park; stand-up paddleboarding in Norway's fjords; try SUP yoga in Boulder, Colorado

A NIGHT AT THE MUSEUM

Dream of exhibits springing to life, or padding slippered feet down corridors bursting with stories: many museums, galleries and zoos offer overnight experiences, a chance to explore hallowed ground after the crowds have left. You might nod off under the belly of a blue whale or amid 3000-year-old Egyptian sculptures, and behind-the-scenes opportunities include laser shows at astronomy centres, historical dress-up or crafting replica artefacts.

1

American Museum of Natural History
New York City, USA

Founded back in 1869, this NY gem contains a veritable wonderland of over 34 million objects, specimens and artefacts – including armies of dinosaur skeletons, herds of stuffed wildlife and a crystal garden of gems and minerals. Adults can stay over for a sophisticated sleepover featuring a champagne reception, dinner, breakfast, live music, a Planetarium show and even a live animal demonstration. The best part? You roll out your sleeping bag under Hall of Ocean Life's iconic blue whale.

Essential information:
Available for those aged 21 and over.

Far left to right: bed down in the fabled galleries of NYC's American Museum of Natural History; sleepover at the Academy of Sciences; tuatara at Wellington Zoo's nocturnal house

2

Wellington Zoo
New Zealand

Committed to conservation, research and captive breeding, Wellington Zoo is home to a menagerie of native and exotic wildlife, including lions and tamarins; the nocturnal house has kiwi and tuatara. From 7pm to 9.30am the place is yours: during Zoo Sleepovers you can help feed and look after the animals, bed down overlooking Monkey Island and join in the morning chores before the doors reopen to the public. A snack and breakfast is included.

Essential information:
Sleeping rolls are provided, but bring your own pillow and sleeping bag or duvet set.

3

Golden Hinde
London, UK

Step aboard this replica of privateer Sir Francis Drake's *Golden Hinde*, the warship that circumnavigated the globe between 1577 and 1580. It's hard to believe that some 60 crew members would have been crammed into such a tiny space. Dress up as a Tudor sailor, become part of the crew and learn how to fire a cannon and navigate before laying your head down on the gun deck. In the morning a Tudor-style breakfast awaits.

Essential information:
The ship's nearest station is London Bridge.

4

California Academy
of Sciences
San Francisco, USA

Ever wondered what 30,000 creatures get up to after dark at the California Academy of Sciences in San Francisco? You can find out on a sleepover at this huge natural history museum. Penguins+Pajamas is for children with adult chaperones or there's adults-only S'mores and Snores, which includes stargazing at the planetarium and breakfast on the living roof. Can't spend the whole night? Attend the NightLife events on Thursday evenings.

Essential information:
Book ahead and check the list of what to bring.

RIDE
A BIKE

Take a day on a bicycle to experience the world at a different pace, freewheeling through beautiful landscapes with the wind in your hair. It doesn't really matter whether you're in France, Finland (left) or somewhere else, the freedom of being on two wheels will transport you wherever you want to go.

MAKE A DATE FOR DANCING

Where words aren't sufficient, get to know the locals on a dancefloor. Whether you're swinging to Cuban salsa in Havana or waltzing in Vienna, a night out dancing lifts the mood like nothing else. Find out where to learn some steps on pages 142-43.

SAVVY WAYS TO SEE THE SUPER-SIGHTS

If you find your bucket list a little unoriginal, try a small sidestep. You don't have to skip the destination entirely – with a bit of foresight, you can make the reality live up to the dream. Plan to see the world's must-see sites in an alternative way, at alternative times. You'll avoid the unadulterated summer-vacation-crowd hell and confirm that savvy-traveller suspicion that the real beauty of superstar landmarks is to see them as seductive mirages from afar.

1

Leaning Tower of Pisa
Italy

Dodge the unromantic scrum of photo-posing and souvenir scouring on Piazza dei Miracoli. Amble instead through medieval backstreets east of the piazza to the Museo dell'Opera del Duomo, and venerate a miraculous mirage of Italy's greatest icon from its back garden – a beautiful cloistered courtyard to boot. The museum is a repository for works of art once displayed in the duomo and baptistry; collection highlights include Giovanni Pisano's ivory carving of the *Madonna and Child* (1299).

Essential information:
Museum tickets include entry to the cathedral bell tower, cupola, baptistry and crypt.

Far left to right: hike the non-renovated Great Wall at Huanghuacheng or Jiankou; get creative to see St Peter's Basilica without the crowds; view London's skyline from a Peckham car park

2

Great Wall of China
China

Before the pandemic struck, stretches of the Great Wall seemed more tourist trap than one of the New Seven Wonders of the World. Instead of enabling this overtourism, a more awe-inspiring approach is to link up with a hiking group to view the Wall snaking through the landscape from afar: the non-renovated Huanghuacheng area features sweeping swaths of Wall that undulate up mountainsides and tumble dramatically into the waters of the Huaijiu River.

Essential information:
Huanghuacheng is less than 2hr from downtown Beijing. Get there via a few buses or split a taxi with a group.

3

London Skyline
Peckham, UK

It doesn't take much to make Londoners happy on a sunny day, and the simple summer-only setup at not-for-profit Frank's Cafe is an alfresco favourite. Leave the crowds and overpriced fare on the South Bank and do as the locals do – jump on a train to South London's trendiest district, Peckham. Drink in the views of London, old and new (and something from the beer taps or cocktail menu), from the top floor of a multistorey car park via pastel-pink stairways, and check out the on-site art.

Essential information:
Frank's is open daily from mid-May to mid-September.

4

St Peter's Basilica
Vatican City, Italy

In the city of outstanding churches, none can hold a candle to St Peter's, Italy's largest, richest and most spectacular basilica. Built atop a 4th-century church, it was consecrated in Rome in 1626 after 120 years of construction. But there's no reason to endure the inevitable crowds here. Find yourself a room with a view, such as a two-bedroom apartment with a staggering – and private – full-frontal of Michelangelo's soaring dome from its 4th-floor perch.

Essential information:
Book early for best availability for apartments such as St Peter's View.

TRAVEL AT HIGH SPEED

From Gare de Lyon, Paris, you can be in Nice or Barcelona in around six hours on France's TGV (Train à Grande Vitesse), speeding through the countryside at more than 300km/h (186mph). Europe and Asia are leading the way in high-speed rail travel that is more sustainable than taking a plane.

THE ART OF RAILWAY TRAVEL

Monisha Rajesh makes peace with her motherland by catching the train.

With a creak and a thud the Island Express to Kanyakumari came to a halt at Kollam Junction – and a canvas bag landed by my lap, followed by a briefcase. As passengers bagged seats by posting bits of luggage through the windows, I was soon surrounded by a family chewing sugar cane, each piece the size of a flute. The youngest smiled, gazing up at me with kohl-rimmed eyes, a tiny bindi between them, and a sticky hand on my knee. She made herself comfortable by the window as her mother produced an additional piece of cane and handed it to me, the area beneath their feet carpeted with husks. In the aisle, a fruit seller squatted on his haunches weighing *sapotas*. He twisted the small furry fruit into paper bags and touched the payment to his forehead before tucking it into the breast pocket of his shirt, eyeing a group of students playing rummy. A few seats away a phone began to play the hit song from the latest Katrina Kaif film, and the train eased away from the platform and continued its journey to the south.

Three months earlier I'd arrived in Chennai with a plan to travel around India in 80 trains. By no means a rail fan, nor an Indophile for that matter, I had long harboured the urge to embrace my motherland and explore it as an unabashed tourist. Born and bred in the UK, I'd lived

in India for two years aged nine, but had never seen the Taj Mahal at dawn, tasted *pani puri* in the backstreets of Bombay or smelled the smoky Delhi air during Diwali. I wanted to watch the reflection of Amritsar's Golden Temple shimmering at night, taste tea in Assam and spot Royal Bengal tigers in Ranthambore – the ultimate Indian bucket list. Brief research made it clear that the cheapest, easiest and most sustainable way to get around the country was by train, with the added benefit that I would meet a microcosm of Indian society on board. How else would I eavesdrop on regular conversations and learn about family feuds, why engineering students want to flee to the US, and why farmers hate the government?

From the outset, I knew this was not a journey of self-discovery. I didn't need to find my roots – which were firmly planted in London – but I wanted to peel back the layers on a dynamic country that seemed to work its magic on everyone who walked its dusty roads and breathed its sweet, warm air, working its way under their skin and settling into their hair. When I was a child, India and I had clashed but I was ready to reassess this relationship and see where I fitted into India and where India fitted in to me. On that first journey, I lay in my berth staring at the ceiling as the train swayed and lurched through the darkness, wondering how I'd manage 79 more trains. There was no real reason for choosing 80, but it set me a task. The idea made me nervous, palm-sweatingly panicked that I might hate it after two rides, but it pushed me far outside my north London comfort zone, and into a frame of mind I'd never had to confront. Carrying more than 23 million passengers a day, Indian Railways is known as the lifeline of the nation, the bloodstream that keeps the country's heart beating – and from the moment I boarded in Chennai, I began to learn why.

Sidled up to the open window, I'd sip my morning tea and watch the show unfold: buffalo snorting in lakes; bent-backed ladies picking tea; young men showering beneath a hose flung over a branch weighed down with blossoms. My trains laid bare the guts of cities, curling around coastlines, skimming cliffs and winding through clouds to the mountains, all the while taking people away from their homes, back to their families, towards new jobs, new lovers, old haunts. On board, the trains gave sanctuary to the tired, the frail, the poor; to the hawker counting his notes after hours of peddling pirated books, plastic rings and combs, or the labourer dozing in his berth after weeks lifting bricks in the sun. And I would watch them as they boarded in groups, teasing one another, laughing, sharing food – four crammed onto a berth made for one.

After four months, 40,000km (24,855 miles) and 80 train journeys, I returned to Chennai and stepped onto the platform, leaving behind the trains that had truly become my home. With their help I'd heard the roar of tigers fighting at Ranthambore, watched the sun rise on the Taj Mahal, tasted bitter tea in Assam and sat in the aura of the Golden Temple at dusk. But above all, I'd slept above strangers, shared their food, watched them work, played with their children and realised, by the end, that the trains had enabled me and India to reconcile our differences and find a way to move on.

ENJOY THE SILENCE

The world's getting louder every day. For a dose of peace and quiet, retreat to an isolated beach, park or desert. Wait until you're out of earshot of the crowds and then feel yourself become absorbed by the quiet. You'll notice that, far from being silent, the natural world in a seemingly empty landscape is full of hushed sounds: a low hum from the bush, the soft wash of surf or a squeak of sand beneath your feet. And it's this near silence that has the capability to bring you the utmost peace.

1

Olympic National Park
Washington, USA

Although it's accessed from Hwy 101, Olympic remains one of the least-peopled national parks in mainland USA, so you can wander without seeing another soul. Most of the park remains relatively untouched by human habitation, with 1000-year-old cedar trees juxtaposed with pristine alpine meadows, clear glacial lakes and a largely roadless interior. Reach the park's coast and the only soundtrack will be the crashing of Pacific surf on wild shores.

Essential information:
The park boasts numerous large, car-accessible campgrounds and around 100 backcountry campsites for overnight excursions.

Far left to right: dunes as far as the eye can see in the Empty Quarter; Hadrian's Wall, Northumberland; Damaraland, Namibia

2

Damaraland
Northwest Namibia

Damaraland is one of the country's last 'unofficial' wildlife regions, and one of the only remaining refuges of the black rhino. Few people live in this ancient landscape and as it's harder to see megafauna, safari parties head elsewhere. There's even a petrified forest and fine prehistoric rock art nearby. You'll likely have the place to yourself – just you and a family of elephants sucking up acacia pods like giant vacuum cleaners.

Essential information:
Guides are compulsory when visiting Twyfelfontein's rock engravings; bear in mind that tips are their only source of income.

3

The Empty Quarter
Arabian Peninsula

Covering 655,000 sq km (25,2897 sq miles) of Saudi Arabia, Oman, the UAE and Yemen, Rub al-Khali spans a fifth of the Arabian Peninsula. Long chains of sculpted dunes reach up to 250m (82ft) high in this 'abode of silence', where cloaks of early morning fog further deaden any sounds. The Bedouin simply call it 'the sands'. You can explore the desert with a 4WD, but be sure to bring all provisions with you.

Essential information:
Arrange overnight stays or trips to the more scenic dunes further in with a tour company or an experienced tour guide.

4

Northumberland
England

Sparsely populated Northumberland National Park is one of England's last true wildernesses. Keep an eye out in the woodlands: this is one of the few places in the country in which to spot red squirrels. Or take a glimpse at some of the world's darkest skies (and the Milky Way) at Kielder Observatory. A section of Hadrian's Wall – the Roman wall running coast-to-coast – also weaves through the park.

Essential information:
Visit April to May and you're sure to see lambs; or come in August when the moors turn purple with flowering heather.

EXPLORE A LOST WORLD

Although you can't travel to space (yet!), you can escape to another world right here on Earth. The secret? Slip below the surface – but not just anywhere. Take it to the extreme. Dip into polar waters. Get under the Outback. Descend into a volcano. Snorkel geothermal lakes and dive concealed cenotes. Beyond the thrill of heading below in aesthetically striking environs, extreme adventures can induce 'adrenaline zen' – a reboot, a sense of tranquillity, and a dose of mindfulness you can bring with you when you resurface.

1

Antarctica

You don't have to go to the ends of the Earth to experience below-the-surface worlds. But if swimming like – and alongside – penguins sounds like a day well spent, then take the ultimate polar plunge on an Antarctic snorkelling or diving excursion. And if dipping into frigid waters to see multi-hued icebergs and the curious inhabitants of this far-flung place – yes, there are sea butterflies, leopard seals and giant isopods – isn't enough to get your heart pumping, perhaps a passing whale will do the trick.

Essential information:
Antarctic snorkelling and diving excursions are available as add-ons to some Antarctic small-ship cruise expeditions.

2

Maldives

Tropical temperatures and abundant marine life make the Maldives a super scuba choice. But here you can witness the world beneath the cerulean surface without ever getting wet. Enclosed underwater offerings include bungalows, restaurants (one with a sub-surface wine cellar) and a DeepFlight submarine. Of course, you should definitely dip more than a toe in: snorkel with manta rays at Hanifaru Bay by day, and cruise the reefs with sharks and stingrays after dark.

Essential information:
A variety of one-day underwater activities are available throughout the Maldives.

3

Southern Australia

With pristine coastlines, pink lakes and rugged Outback ranges, this state is certainly gorgeous. But it's the below-surface surprises that set it apart. At Coober Pedy's underground city, residents live in 'dugouts' – and you can dine, sleep and attend church beneath the scorched earth. Or grab a snorkel and go sinkhole-hopping near Mount Gambier, where cave systems have water so clear and chasms so striking that you'll feel you're floating in space without leaving Earth.

Essential information:
Fly direct from Adelaide to Mount Gambier or Coober Pedy; you can also add a Coober Pedy excursion to journeys on The Ghan train.

4

Iceland

Experience Earth's extremes in the 'Land of Fire and Ice'. This is the only place on the planet where – in just one day – you can descend 120m (400ft) into a dormant volcano to explore the colourful, 4000-year-old Þríhnúkagígur magma chamber; snorkel over active geothermal hot-spring vents at Kleifarvatn Lake; and dive into the icy glacial waters between two tectonic plates at Silfra fissure in Unesco World Heritage-listed Þingvellir National Park.

Essential information: Þríhnúkagígur volcano, Kleifarvatn Lake and Silfra fissure are all less than a 1hr drive from Reykjavík, Iceland's capital city.

Clockwise, from top: swim with gentoo penguins in Antarctica; bed down in a Coober Pedy dugout, Australia; diving deep waters at Silfra fissure, Iceland

"THIS GRAND SHOW IS
SUNRISE SOMEWHERE;
DRIED AT ONCE; A SHOWER
VAPOR IS EVER RISING.
SUNSET, ETERNAL DAWN
AND CONTINENTS AND
TURN, AS THE ROUND

ETERNAL. IT IS ALWAYS
THE DEW IS NEVER ALL
IS FOREVER FALLING;
ETERNAL SUNRISE, ETERNAL
AND GLOAMING, ON SEA
SLANDS, EACH IN ITS
EARTH ROLLS."

– JOHN MUIR, *JOHN OF THE MOUNTAINS:*
THE UNPUBLISHED JOURNALS OF JOHN MUIR

SEE THE SUNSET

Put the camera down, there
are enough snaps of sunsets in
the world already. Instead, sit in
stillness and just watch. Reflect
on the day that is in the process
of becoming yesterday, and what
tomorrow will bring. Sunsets are
a daily reminder of the passage
of time. The average person will
see tens of thousands of sunsets,
but every now and then, go
somewhere spectacular, such as
Arches National Park in Utah, and
make one count.

SAVOUR DARK SKIES

Join a Star Party at the McDonald Observatory in Texas, where the wonders of the cosmos are celebrated in a friendly environment. Many observatories offer similar events but alternatively you could also visit one of several Dark Sky Parks on a clear night.

CLIMB A VOLCANO

Volcanoes ignite something in us all. Feel the heat and connect with the deepest reaches of our little planet. Arrive at the summit and you've reached the top of the world. Stretching below, the volcano's shadow creeps across the landscape. The perfectly formed crater might be quiet for now, gently puffing out smoke or, at its most dramatic, bubbling with lava at its core. Take a day to hike to the top and breathe in its life, whether long-gone or slumbering.

1

Mt Fuji
Japan

Of all Japan's iconic images, Mt Fuji (3776m/11,076ft) is the real deal. Admiration for the mountain appears in Japan's earliest recorded literature, dating from the 8th century. And, like volcanoes all around the world, Mt Fuji is sacred: Buddhists call it the 'Peak of the White Lotus'. Hundreds make it to the summit every day during the July and August climbing season, resting for the night in mountain huts. Find true solitude with a winter ascent.

Essential information:
It's a gruelling climb, busy in the climbing season. You can walk the 4km (2.4-mile) circumference of the crater, but it may be clouded over.

Far left to right: Japan's iconic Mt Fuji; a bird's eye view of Mt St Helens, Washington; Ecuador's glacier-draped Cotopaxi

2

Kīlauea
Hawai'i, USA

Kīlauea is arguably the world's most active volcano, having erupted almost continuously since 1983 – at one point filling a lava lake at 403 million gallons (1525 million litres) per second. Do the 7km (4.5-mile) loop counterclockwise through an astounding microcosm of Hawai'i Volcanoes National Park, descending through ohia forests to the lava lake at the summit caldera, with views of flowing lava and ash clouds.

Essential information:
Hit the trail before 8am to beat the crowds. The faint footpath across the crater floor is marked by *ahu* (stone cairns) to aid navigation.

3

Mt St Helens
Washington, USA

Part of the Pacific Rim of Fire, Mt St Helens' towering 2549m (8363ft) peak reigns over the lush and lofty Cascade Mountains. Most famous for its ruthless 1980 steam explosion, which killed scores of people and rained ash across the world, the volcano had hitherto been dormant since 1857. Make out the edge of the blast zone by the long-dead trees, still standing upright in stark contrast to the undamaged old-growth forests.

Essential information:
The beautiful peak can be climbed in a day. Spring to fall is best for climbing, though it's accessible to hikers year-round.

4

Cotopaxi
Ecuador

Dominating Ecuador's central highlands with its glacier-draped cone and smoking fumaroles, this 5897m-high (19,347ft) volcano promises an accessible high-altitude climb. After acclimatising at 4800m (15,748ft), you leave the climber's refuge at midnight, stepping out in a headlamp glow across a moonscape of snow, shadow, rock and ravine. You'll don crampons and ice axe, and rope up when you hit the glacier.

Essential information:
It's a six- to eight-hour mission past crevasses and hanging seracs toward the invisible summit.

CHAPTER 3

A WEEK

LEARN A PRACTICAL SKILL

Whether it's learning how to service your own car, cook sustainably, perform first aid or do some basic plumbing, a week is just enough time to pick up the basics of a practical skill. Also, you can take a course almost anywhere around the world and then pass on the know-how.

HIT THE ROAD

Road trips take many forms, from adventures and escapes to quests for meaning. But one theme unites them all: freedom! You're (literally) in the driving seat, free to make impromptu detours, impulsive itinerary changes, to snack at all hours. Whether you go solo or with friends, you can experience a multitude of destinations in a short space of time, as well as the romantic anonymity that comes with road tripping. Rock up somewhere new, swap stories with locals, then move on – a mysterious stranger, never to return...

1

Ruta 40
Argentina

If you drove coast to coast across the USA, you still wouldn't match the length of mighty Ruta 40. At 5000km (3107 miles), this is Argentina's longest road, and it links glaciers, forests, deserts and salt-flats. Some travellers keep it short, and embark on a lake-spangled circuit from Bariloche and back again. But tackling 'La Cuarenta' in her entirety leads you along winding mountain roads in El Bolsón to ruggedly rocky Piedra Parada and the stately forests of Parque Nacional Los Alerces.

Essential information: For flower-dappled views, drive the Ruta in late spring/summer (November to December). Begin in Bariloche, a 2hr flight from capital Buenos Aires.

2

Kyoto to Tsunoshima
Japan

Bullet trains are Japan's iconic mode of transport. But road-tripping this route doesn't only lead you through western Honshū's most celebrated cities: it offers remarkable views you can only see by car. After experiencing Kyoto's temples and Osaka's all-night karaoke bars, you'll head west along roads lined with maple trees. Beyond Hiroshima's museums and memorials, you'll reach the climax of the 584km (363-mile) drive: a dramatic bridge crossing that leads to the lush crags of Tsunoshima Island.

Essential information: Rent a car from multiple spots at Kyoto station or the international airport. Set your navigation app before leaving, as rural areas have no English signage.

3

Transfăgărășan
Romania

From above, Romania's daredevil Transfăgărășan looks like an erratic zigzag scoured across the Făgăraș Mountains. Erstwhile dictator Ceaușescu constructed this 151km (94-mile) road as a strategic route connecting Wallachia to Transylvania. It's an engineering marvel with jaw-dropping viaducts, hundreds of bridges, and tunnels including the 890m-long (2920ft) Capra-Bâlea. Despite the white-knuckle hairpins, it's well maintained for a mountain road – but take it slow and beware high winds.

Essential information: Start from the south in busy Bucharest, or from the north in Sibiu or Brașov. Travel between July and October: the road is only fully open for half the year.

4

Great River Road
USA

Want a great American road trip, but on a road less travelled than Route 66 or the Pacific Coast Highway? The Great River Road follows the mighty Mississippi from Minnesota right to the Gulf of Mexico, spanning 4800km (2982 miles) and 10 states. There are historic sights, outdoor activities and roadside oddities aplenty, so you can choose your own adventure: the childhood home of Johnny Cash, endless opportunities for barbecue, and multiple sections crowned as National Scenic Byways.

Essential information: Allow 10 days to do the whole drive. Highlights are the Twin Cities of Minneapolis and St Paul; historic Dubuque; Iowa; and rock 'n' roll Memphis.

VISIT LITERARY LOCATIONS

Reading a book is like travel for the mind. Through a book, you can immerse yourself in another place – and perhaps be inspired to travel there, too. After closing its pages, you might want to gaze up at the cathedral immortalised in Victor Hugo's *The Hunchback of Notre-Dame*, or experience the vibrancy of Nigeria as depicted in Chimamanda Ngozi Adichie's *Purple Hibiscus*. Of course, every author adds their own interpretation to a place. That just means you'll have to see for yourself, using your imagination as a guide.

Dublin, Ireland
Normal People by Sally Rooney

Rooney's heartrending depiction of self-conscious young lovers has an elegant setting in Dublin, and it's easy for readers to retrace Connell and Marianne's steps: Trinity College landmarks include the Campanile and libraries. The lovers' hometown, Carricklea, is fictional; get a glimpse of their isolated rural upbringing in Sligo County's windswept Streedagh Strand, where parts of the TV adaptation were filmed.

Essential information: Ferries reach Dublin from Liverpool and Holyhead; or you can jump on a flight from myriad European airports.

Far left to right: Trinity College Old Library, Dublin; Tasmania's Franklin River; Knossos in Crete, the island home of Circe's sister (and mother of the Minotaur) Pasiphaë

2

Malibu, California, USA
Malibu Rising by Taylor Jenkins Reid

'Malibu' conjures up blonde beaches and opulent mansions, with a whisper of scandal – the perfect setting for this explosive novel. Travel in late summer for the full effect: in the novel, this is when the secrets of the beautiful, wealthy Riva siblings reach a fiery conclusion. Wriggle your toes on sandy Zuma Beach, and eavesdrop at beachside cafes... you never know what secret lives you might uncover.

Essential information:
The novel's oceanfront mansion lifestyle will cost you a few grand; you could also day-trip to Malibu from a base in LA.

3

Tasmania, Australia
Death of a River Guide by Richard Flanagan

The merciless Australian bush is as much a character in Flanagan's novel as its main protagonist, Aljaz, whose life flashes before his eyes as he drowns on a river ride, his death a mere a footnote to the novel's story of his ancestors. Your own Franklin River rafting trip will be without incident – but you'll be immersed in Flanagan's setting, from thrashing rapids to teeming rainforest.

Essential information:
Ferries and planes link Melbourne to Tasmania. From there, you'll need a car or private transfer to Franklin River.

4

Mediterranean islands, Europe
Circe by Madeline Miller

Homer's *Odyssey* made a popular comeback in this retelling, focused on enigmatic half-goddess and witch Circe. Ancient myth and modern fiction collide in the novel, so it isn't easy to tread her footsteps. But island-hopping the Aeolians will give you a taste of Aeaea, to where Circe was banished; cypress-dotted Crete is where Circe visited her sister, Pasiphaë, mother of the Minotaur.

Essential information:
There are no ferries connecting Crete and the Aeolians, but Athens and Naples are the best jumping-off points.

"I FELT MY LUNGS THE ONRUSH AIR, MOUNTAINS, I THOUGHT, WHAT IT IS TO

INFLATE WITH
OF SCENERY –
TREES, PEOPLE.
'THIS IS
BE HAPPY.'"

– SYLVIA PLATH, *THE BELL JAR*

STAY IN A TREEHOUSE

Sweet dreams are made of this: relive your childhood in a room above a forest floor. Even better – when you're bedding down in a forest-swathed abode, the hard work of construction has been done for you. Sleeping suspended amid the trees, you're closer to the elements, the wind rushing through the branches, the rain pounding on the roof, birds both seen and heard. For a few days a year, get back to nature and curl up in one of these leafy boltholes.

1

Châteaux dans les Arbes
Dordogne, France

As if a secluded hideaway in the trees wasn't enough of a childhood dream come true, at Châteaux dans les Arbes in the Dordogne, the leafy abodes are also wooden replicas of the neighbouring medieval castles. Housed around the former moat of a ruined stronghold, the three creations are the handiwork of veteran treehouse-builder Rémi, complete with turrets and spires. On-site there's an outdoor pool, playground, restaurant and bikes for exploring this historic area.

Essential information:
The treehouse castles are 30min from Bergerac Airport.

2

Free Spirit Spheres
Vancouver Island, Canada

Suspended by a web of ropes in the temperate rainforest canopy of Vancouver Island, these smooth wooden spheres are designed to coexist with their surroundings, with minimum impact on the trees and wildlife. Compact two- to three-person pods have pull-down beds, built-in cabinets and mini-libraries. Creature comforts, including bathrooms and a sauna, are back on solid ground; beyond the forest are the Cowichan Valley's wineries and artisanal eateries.

Essential information:
The spheres are 18km (11 miles) northwest of Qualicum Beach, but are well hidden in the forest. Book ahead and ask for directions.

3

Chole Mjini
Chole, Tanzania

This cluster of seven treehouses is cradled by baobab trees on Chole, a tropical island east of the Tanzanian coast. Perched amongst vegetation and crumbling ruins, the upmarket thatched huts are electricity-free and far removed from urban life. Eat fresh seafood, gaze up at clear stars and explore local dive sites in the knowledge that a portion of Chole Mjini's earnings are channelled into local community projects like a clinic, kindergarten and a school.

Essential information:
Regular flights connect nearby Mafia with most airports in Tanzania - from Dar Es Salaam, flying time is around 30min.

4

Bangkok Treehouse
Bang Krachao, Thailand

Turbocharged Bangkok makes an unexpectedly tranquil treehouse location. In the city's southeast, Bang Krachao is a near-island carved by a loop of the Chao Phraya River, a place of mangrove, palm and fruit trees, threaded with waterways, semi-rural villages and ancient temples. Presiding over the river, these midair hideaways, made from recycled and sustainable materials, come with thoughtful amenities like movie-loaded private computers, bike use and free ice-cream.

Essential information: The treehouses are a 10min walk from Bangnamphueng Nok Temple.

Clockwise, from top: Châteaux dans les Arbes, Dordogne; Bangkok Treehouse, Thailand; Vancouver's Free Spirit Spheres, Canada

LEARN TO DANCE

Get your steps straight in one of the world's dance capitals. Whether you're a smooth mover or the clumsy owner of two left feet, nothing can compare to getting to the roots of a dance in its home country. You'll learn the history, appreciate the passion and culture and, with any luck, take your newfound expertise home with you. And no one can ever tell you that you 'can't dance' when you know you've learnt from the very best in the world.

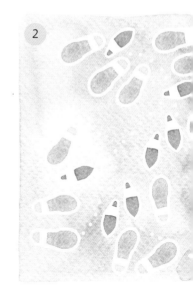

1

Lindy hop
New York City, USA

Evolving in the Black communities of Harlem in the 1920s and '30s, the Lindy hop was instrumental in breaking the race barrier at the Savoy Ballroom, one of few racially integrated dance halls of the era. A fusion of jazz, tap, breakaway and Charleston, the Lindy hop's most recognisable moves are the swing-out and air-step. There's no denying its global resurgence, but for real authenticity, go back to where it all began at the Harlem Swing Dance Society for events, tours and classes.

Essential information:
Harlem Swing Dance Society offer walking, van or bus tours, and can arrange student and private tours.

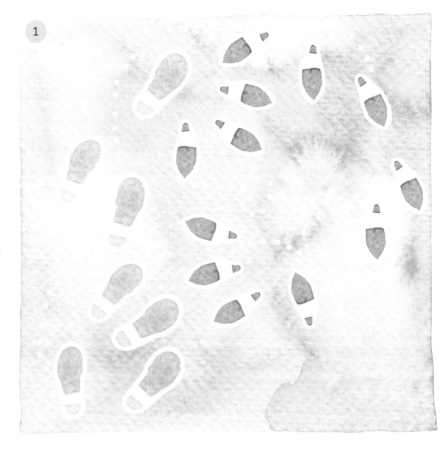

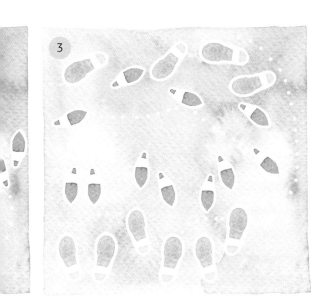

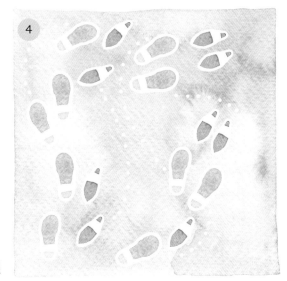

2

Waltz
Vienna, Austria

Originating as a folk dance in the Austrian suburbs, the Viennese waltz slightly anticipates the second beat, making it that bit faster than other waltzes. And what better way to glide in three-quarter time than by the Danube River to Johann Strauss' *Blue Danube Waltz*? In fact, ditch *Auld Lang Syne* and see in the New Year the romantic Austrian way, waltzing to Strauss; the Elmayer Dance School will also teach dance manners and etiquette!

Essential information: Elmayer is located in the Palais Pallavicini's former stables, next to the Spanish Riding School stables.

3

Salsa
Havana, Cuba

So you think you can salsa? Then you're in for a surprise in Havana, baby. The indefatigable Cuban salsa energy ricochets off walls and emanates most emphatically from the people dancing it. Also known as *casino* (the Spanish for dance hall), Cuba's salsa has its origins in flirtation and is a lot more rotational than salsa taught elsewhere in the world. It features a strong leader with a push-pull style – ideal for learners. Tradition requires the music being 'felt' rather than necessarily following a beat.

Essential information: Take your salsa classes at Old Havana's Casa del Son.

4

Tango
Buenos Aires, Argentina

The tango's history began in the bars and brothels of BA's colourful La Boca port area. Here, immigrants from Europe mingled their own musical traditions with local rhythms like *candombe*, which arrived about a century earlier with enslaved Africans. The rhythm and lyrics combined to symbolise the plaintive cry of the homesick immigrant, the jilted lover's bitter lament and the *porteño*'s hymn to Buenos Aires. Eschew the public displays and dinner shows for the city's many *milongas* (tango dance halls).

Essential information: Try the city's Escuela del Tango for classes.

HIDDEN IN PLAIN SIGHT

Not every amazing sight will find its way into a travel guidebook. Indeed, some have been forgotten about completely. Even in cities, there are mysterious places under and above ground. We've all heard of India's Taj Mahal, but what about Rajasthan's Karni Mata Temple? It's a building teeming with rats so revered they enjoy A-list treatment with daily offerings of milk and fruit. Similarly, it's no secret that visitors to Berlin can see parts of its infamous Wall still standing in the city. Not so many people know that segments of the Wall have travelled all around the world and can be found as far away as Japan and Iceland. Or discover the fertile abandoned-building hunting ground of the former Soviet republics; check out the concrete war memorials built in the 1960s and 1970s in the former Yugoslavia. The most fascinating finds often happen to exist right in front of our very eyes.

GO UPRIVER

Rivers offer intrigue and adventure, consistency and unpredictability – there are few more accurate metaphors for life. Go with the flow and float downstream or take on the currents and head upstream, such as here in Laos.

EXPLORE ANCIENT RUINS

Nothing takes you out of your own galaxy like exploring ancient ruins – poking about nosily, venerating lost artworks, reconsidering your cultural understanding IRL. And just as happened at the ash-covered homes of Pompeii or the Maya ruins of Tikal in the Guatemalan jungle, these abandoned places untether us from the egoic. They remove us from the notion that we are at the centre of the universe, or at the peak of human understanding. Instead, dazzled by their wonder, they remind us of but one thing: civilisation's fragility.

1

Angkor Wat
Cambodia

Shrouded by thick jungle for centuries, Angkor Wat is the daddy among a series of ancient temples rediscovered near Siem Reap in 1860. Still the world's largest religious building, it carries Cambodia's national pride within carvings and motifs such as the evocative Churning of the Ocean of Milk bas-relief. But no amount of religious devotion could save the temple from the elements. Damaged irreparably by drought and monsoon, it was left abandoned.

Essential information:
The jewel of Angkor Archaeological Park, Angkor Wat is 6km (4 miles) north of Siem Reap; get there by taxi, *moto* or *remork*.

Far left to right: Petra's vast Monastery, Jordan; Tikal's Templo V, Guatemala; Ta Prohm, jungle-wreathed jewel of Angkor Archaeological Park

2

Tikal
Guatemala

Hidden in the tropical folds of Reserva de la Biosfera Maya, Tikal was the Maya world's HQ. Today, its mighty plazas and palaces still stand, littered with monumental sculptures; park campers can climb the tallest pyramid, Templo IV, for front-row sunrise seats. Though human sacrifice likely took place here, it didn't appease the gods enough to stop long periods of drought – thought to be the reason for Tikal's abandonment.

Essential information:
Most visit Tikal by day trip from El Remate or Flores; overnight for more time with the temples and the resident agoutis and monkeys.

3

Pompeii
Italy

Crushed, boiled or asphyxiated – such was the terrible fate of Pompeii's citizens when Mt Vesuvius blew in 79 CE. But their bad luck was our good fortune: the city's sudden burial served to protect it from vandalism, looting and the weather for 1700 years. Pompeii's most compelling remnant is the original graffiti: from insults to election notices, these scribblings give a direct line into ancient Roman life.

Essential information:
Pompeii's ruins are best reached by trains to Pompei Scavi-Villa dei Misteri station (36min from Naples; 30min from Sorrento).

4

Petra
Jordan

The first glimpse of the great Nabataean Kingdom capital flips your wig. Arriving via high-sided, narrow Al Siq Canyon, the Treasury appears, a grandiose masterwork of Corinthian columns and intricate reliefs carved out of red sandstone cliffs. With its vast Theatre, Monastery and Silk Tomb, the Rose City still wows like it's 312 BCE – a reminder that after we're gone, the marks we leave behind remain for millennia.

Essential information:
Petra is accessible by bus/ minibus from Wadi Rum (2hr), Aqaba (2.5hr) and Amman (4hr). Driving shaves 30min from all journey times.

GET WILD
AND CAMP
OFF-GRID

Emily Matchar gets away from the everyday in the wilderness.

The weather report had made mention of rain, but my friend Allison and I – desperate to get out of town after a stressful work week – had ignored it. 'It'll be a sprinkle,' we told each other. 'Just a little mist!' Now we were 3000m (10,000ft) above sea level in New Mexico's Pecos Wilderness, trapped in our tent as a thunderstorm raged overhead.

The way up, at least, had been delightful. We'd spent the day cutting switchbacks through the deep-green spruce forest, Allison's dogs clambering ahead, tails wagging with joy. We'd crossed a long ridge with shivery-beautiful views of the Sangre de Cristo Mountains, then descended slightly into an alpine meadow spangled with late-summer wildflowers. The sky was that clear dark blue of New Mexico September, all haze burned away by the high-altitude sun. There wasn't a single cloud. Until there was.

Fortunately we'd had time to pitch our tent before the rains started. At first they were fat lazy drops, but they quickly became that hard stinging rain that feels like shot pellets, driving sideways on a suddenly icy wind. We weren't totally unprepared; we'd brought a rain fly and tarps. It was monsoon season, after all, when New Mexico's high desert sees frequent afternoon showers.

But usually those showers end quickly, the sky innocently blue again within an hour. Not today. Today we were stuck in the tent as thunder echoed through the mountain valleys. The two dogs had grown squirrelly, and were circling each other in the enclosed space, leaving muddy pawprints across our sleeping bags. There's a reason why I do this, I reminded myself.

That's the difference between car camping and tent camping: the unpredictability. No shade on car camping: who doesn't love rolling up to site with a well-stocked trunk – inflatable mattresses, lanterns, a radio, a Dutch oven for making chocolate-cherry dump cake? But that comfort means the adventure is muffled. There's less room for chance. If it rains, you can always pack it up and find the nearest motel. Forget the canned cherries for your cake? Drive to the nearest supermarket.

Wild camping in a tent forces you to confront your unconscious reliance on convenience and stimulation: food at the touch of a phone screen; TV shows on demand anytime; a million books to download with a single click.

Stuck in the tent, Allison and I had only one paperback novel between us. So we got creative: I used my Swiss Army knife to slice the book in two, giving Allison the half I had already finished. When we got done with that, we played cards for hours, laughing so much the dogs looked at us quizzically. Since you can't use a camp stove in a tent (well, you shouldn't!), we had to scrap our planned meal and dine on granola bars and wax-wrapped cheese snacks instead. I fell asleep listening to the wind whistle and the rain patter, my mind so much sharper than during an average night when I drift off listening to podcasts or scrolling through my phone.

We woke to a sparkling and cold mountain morning. Summer had seemingly turned into fall overnight. It only took a mile or two to forget the wet mess of the past 18 hours. We hiked above the timberline, the smell of ice in the air. We descended into a steep canyon cut through with a clear alpine stream, the dogs lapping eagerly at the fresh water. Our next campsite was at a lower elevation, on a soft forest floor amidst clean-smelling firs. I fell asleep before the sun had fully set, feeling somehow purified, as if the residue of daily living had been washed away by the rain and the cold air.

Here's the other great thing about wild camping: by the time you get out of the wilderness, civilization seems amazing. The best pizza I ever had was a soggy Pizza Hut pie after a sweaty trek along the floor of the Grand Canyon. The end of this camping trip with Allison was no different. When we found our car at the trailhead, we went straight to the gas station and stuffed ourselves with fake-cheese-coated chips and low-quality chocolate. Delectable. Then, still chilled from the altitude, we drove to a local hot spring, where we bobbed like seals in the steaming, mineral-scented water. I love a hot spring any time, but after several days of walking through the mountains with a pack on my back: heaven. You know what else was heaven? My bed that night. I didn't even need to scroll through my phone to fall asleep.

Sometimes you need to get away from the everyday to remind yourself of just how lovely ordinary life is. And when you start to forget again? The wilderness is there, waiting.

DOORSTEP DISCOVERY

Nicola Williams learns to love what's local

As the last of the sun's rays blazed across the water before sinking behind the dark mountains beyond, the old-fashioned wooden schooner sliced through pink reflections. Red sails tangoed in the soft summer breeze and we lazed in their shade, sipping the last of our champagne. And to think this was right on my doorstep, on the southern shore of Lake Geneva.

Several months prior, I'd taken a tumble, broken my back, and was trussed up in a brace for the best part of a year. Travel per se was not prohibited – but planes, trains and automobiles were. If I was to go anywhere, my internal compass would require a dramatic reboot.

Monday

My culinary curiosity was the first to succumb. All too soon my ritual morning stroll wound up at the village *boucherie* (butcher's shop), where golden roast chickens tantalised on a spit outside and the line snaked out the door on Sunday mornings. I grilled the butcher for his culinary secrets, smugly leaving with several veal slices and his recipe for *paupiettes de veau* (veal roulades) simmered in local Savoie wine.

Tuesday

I walked to the neighbouring village to buy fish direct from the fisherman. I'd often watched his boat cross the lake from my kitchen window, a lonesome speck returning home from a pre-dawn voyage to empty out crayfish pots and nets swimming with silvery perch and féra. But it took perseverance to find the unpaved lane leading to his house on the shore. The passion with which Madame, deftly filleting the catch, explained how to create the perfect oil, lemon and garlic marinade to douse over her legendary hand-cut *carpaccio de féra* was humbling and overwhelming.

Wednesday

I started devouring signs. I learnt that the Espace Litorelle, our village hall, which had caused such a rumpus at the time with its radically contemporary facade, was named after *la litorelle* (*Littorella uniflora*), a rare and protected aquatic plant with tiny cream flowers that has grown for centuries on Lake Geneva's shores.

Thursday

Indulging one's inner child is an essential part of travel, even on one's very own doorstep: hence the day I

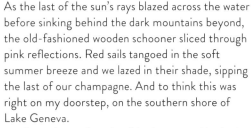

discovered the Chemin des Douaniers, an overgrown footpath that snaked from the public beach into thick woods. Ten minutes' stumbling over tree roots in the half-dark rewarded with brilliant blue sunshine, a Dolby Surround view of the open water and a clear footpath that curled as far as the eye could see along the lake's pebbled shore. This secret lakeside path, a voyeur's peephole on the lavish villas bejewelling Lake Geneva, was pure gold.

Friday

As summer bit the dust and the rains came, I found myself tramping with the local farmer's wife through soggy oak and hornbeam woods in search of mushrooms: wild boletus, golden chanterelles and nutty tasting trumpets of death (not deadly, I quickly learnt). Forget jetting off to Italy to hunt truffles or to Japan to search for shiitake – the sudden grassroots intimacy I was experiencing with my home was revelatory.

Saturday

And so I came to sail *La Licorne*, a magnificent grand dame of a double-mast schooner that had worked the seas as a fishing vessel in the 1960s, perfectly capping off my local voyage of discovery.

SADDLE UP FOR HORSEPACKING

Giddy up! Pick a steed, slide into the saddle and spend a week in some tough terrain that will have you contemplating your existence in no time. It's accepted – no, expected – that you'll use this sojourn in the saddle to let the larger-than-life vistas give you healthy perspective. Your phone firmly tucked away, you're aware that the only thing you'll be notified by is your horse when she's hungry or tired. Tune into her as she plods steadily into the wilds.

1

Fazenda Catuçaba
Brazil

Perched atop the Serra do Mar mountain range some 70km (43 miles) from Ubatuba, this charming former coffee *fazenda* (estate) is now a boutique hotel, celebrating rural Brazil's equestrian culture via guided trail rides of varying lengths, suited to different ages and levels of ability. The sprawling surrounds hold coffee and sugar-cane plantations, a lake and an outdoor art gallery, and bird walks or kayaking trips are also on offer.

Essential information:
You're expected to switch off at the *fazenda*: there is no mobile phone signal or internet access, and no televisions on site.

Far left to right: a winter excursion from Triple Creek Ranch; ride with Mongolia's nomads on an Equitours trek; your mount awaits at La Morada de los Andes

2

Triple Creek Ranch
USA

Horse riding is a year-round activity at this Montana Rockies hideaway in the Bitterroot range: trek through pine forests, wildflower meadows or freshly fallen snow. From June to September, riders can take part in cattle drives, although conditions are rather more luxurious than is traditional, with gourmet packed lunches and a swimming pool or hot tub waiting at the end.

`Essential information:`
`Find Triple Creek in Darby,`
`Montana, just under 2hr`
`from Missoula, from where`
`you can arrange transfers.`

3

Equitours
Worldwide

Equitours has 40 years of experience organising horseback vacations for riders of all abilities in far-flung destinations. Guests might gallop with zebras in Kenya, ride with nomads in Mongolia, drive cattle in Wyoming or saunter through vineyards in France. Choose from a variety of ride activities, from polo to beach or mountain treks, and know that the trips support local initiatives like Kenya's DSWT wildlife conservation organization.

`Essential information:`
`Rate your riding ability`
`and reserve a place on a`
`ride online.`

4

La Morada de los Andes
Argentina to Chile

In Mendoza's Uco Valley you're in the heart of Argentine wine country, and every February, the La Morada de los Andes winery – based in a 270-hectare (667-acre) vineyard – hosts a luxury residential community here. Guests can stay for a five-night Gourmet Andes Crossing through the mountains to Santiago. The riding is hard, but the wine flows freely. The stay is complete with garden, pool and outdoor terraces looking out to the snowcapped mountain tops.

`Essential information:`
`The La Morada winery is`
`418km (260 miles) from`
`Santiago, Chile.`

"SOME
I AM MORE
THAN
AND I AM
HOW TO STOP
FOR MY

DAYS
WOLF
WOMAN
STILL LEARNING
APOLOGISING
WILD."

– NIKITA GILL, 'WOLF AND WOMAN'

SUSTAINABLE SAFARIS

We are so keen to encounter animals that we travel great distances to wander where wild things roam. It's a little mad, but it also might be completely natural. According to modern-day Darwin, EO Wilson, our attraction to nature and living things is innate. And it comes with a bonus: being in the wild forces you out of your head and into the moment – fertile grounds for a reset. So, book that safari, and be sure to choose an outfitter with ethical practices and a commitment to conservation.

1

Sabi Sabi
South Africa

With no fence separating this private game reserve from the Kruger National Park, big game – and yes, that includes the Big 5 – is free to pass through. Wild is woven into every moment at Sabi Sabi: sip your morning coffee while a herd of elephants drink from a watering hole nearby. Watch lions catch an afternoon catnap. Spot hyenas slinking through the darkness. Soak in a tub with views of the bushveld, and dine on local eats under the stars.

Essential information:
Sabi Sabi is a 1hr flight from OR Tambo International Airport in Johannesburg, South Africa.

2

Churchill Wild
Manitoba, Canada

Side effects of embarking on the only walking safari in polar bear territory may include a sense of awe and 'awww' – these captivating creatures are simultaneously fierce and fetching. No two experiences are exactly alike in this remote wilderness on the edge of the Arctic, each day dictated by weather and wildlife movement, and each evening a potential opportunity to bathe in the enchanting, electric blaze of the aurora borealis, which appears here 300 days per year.

Essential information:
Churchill Wild's lodges and safari experiences are reachable by bush plane from Churchill, Manitoba.

3

Pugdundee Safaris
Central India

Tread lightly through the rugged terrain of Satpura Tiger Reserve on a trip with Central India's pioneers of walking safaris. But stay alert; although this is a lesser-known park and the hike through the jungle can be meditative, you're walking in the wild and Satpura is home to tigers, leopards, wild boar, crocodiles, bison, sloth bears and more. If you prefer solid walls rather than swag camps at night, you can opt instead for one of Pugdundee's eco-lodge-based safaris.

Essential information:
The closest airport to Pugdundee Safaris and its eco-lodges is in Bhopal, Madhya Pradesh.

4

Cottar's Safaris
Kenya

Tucked between Kenya's Maasai Mara and Tanzania's Serengeti National Park, the sole safari camp in Olderkesi Conservancy offers the chance to contribute to conservation and witness the Great Migration – without the crowds. Bush walks and game drives immerse you in the rich biodiversity; 'Impact Experiences' connect you with people: take a medicinal walk with a hunter-gatherer or join a ranger for a day at the only Maasai Mara camp to employ an all-female ranger unit.

Essential information: Cottar's Private Airstrip is a 40min flight from Wilson Airport in Nairobi, Kenya.

Clockwise, from top: book a sustainable safari to spot polar bears, leopards, elephants and more in the wild

SET JETTING

Binge-streaming your favourite show is a great way to escape, but you can follow your imagination even further by planning a TV-themed trip. The trick is to capture a flavour of the setting, rather than ticking off sights you saw in the series. This way, you can avoid contributing to overtourism – steering well clear of *Game of Thrones* crowds in Dubrovnik, or New York's *Sex and the City* tour buses – and let the ambiance wash over you instead.

1

Madrid, Spain,
Money Heist

Red boilersuits, Dalí masks and Madrid's palatial architecture give crime drama *La Casa de Papel* (*Money Heist*) a distinctive aesthetic. In a bid to steal millions from Spain's Royal Mint, robbers duck behind marble columns and taunt the police from grand staircases, while secrets are divulged in hole-in-the-wall cafes. Royal Mint scenes were filmed at the Spanish National Research Council; gang mastermind Professor Salvador revealed his ingenious plan at Torrelodones.

Essential information:
Zoom straight to Madrid from London by taking the Eurostar to Paris, followed by a direct train.

Far left to right: immerse in Madrid's *Money Heist* intrigue; find peak *Twin Peaks* at Snoqualmie Falls; follow *Big Little Lies* to Old Fisherman's Wharf, Monterey

2

California, USA
Big Little Lies

Coastal Monterey is so postcard-perfect that it almost feels like a simulation, so it's the ideal setting for *Big Little Lies*, whose characters battle to project perfection despite their deeply buried secrets. They gossip over brunch at Old Fisherman's Wharf, idle through Monterey Bay Aquarium and drive coastal Hwy 1. Plunge deeper into their world by driving past Carmel Highlands mansions or to dramatic Garrapata State Park Beach.

Essential information:
Rent a car for the full wind-in-your-hair experience, or take a train or bus from San Francisco.

3

South Korea
Squid Game

Its bloodthirsty premise is simple – win the prize, or lose your life – and *Squid Game*'s morally ambiguous characters, betrayals and intrigues won it legions of viewers. The games unfold on a secret island lair that has been pinned down to Seongapdo; eschew this uninhabited isle for a similarly lonesome island beauty via a ferry from Incheon to Deokjeokdo. Die-hard fans head to Seoul's Sangbong Bus Terminal to replicate antihero Gi-hun's gambling scenes.

Essential information:
Singapore Airlines and Thai Airways fly to Seoul. From there, train services take you west to Incheon.

4

Washington State, USA
Twin Peaks

Eerie, mountainous and shrouded in mist: *Twin Peaks*' main filming locations heighten the unsettling ambience of this 1990s cult drama, and Washington has embraced its status as a David Lynch pilgrimage site. Snap a picture at the Kiana Lodge beach where Laura Palmer's body was found; or feel the mist from Snoqualmie Falls, topped by the Great Northern Hotel. And, of course, local haunts offer 'damn fine coffee' and cherry pie.

Essential information:
Locations are in easy reach of Seattle, which you can reach from LA via the Coast Starlight train.

COAST TO COAST

From sea to shining sea: there's more than one way to cross a country. When you consider your preferred mode of transport and how you choose to tackle the terrain, travelling the full span of a nation is as easy or hard as you make it. Either way, this is the type of trip that refuses to be rushed. Going slow is the only way to take in the gradual – or dramatic – changes in the landscape. Just one more hill...

1

England by bike

Each year, some 12–15,000 cyclists cross some of the more rugged stretches of the country via the Sea to Sea (C2C) cycle route across northern England, huffing and puffing their way over the Pennines – England's spine – via the northern Lake District National Park. But as you pedal up Whinlatter Pass, before stopping at the 4500-year-old Castlerigg stone circle near Keswick, you may be thankful that this route across England's northern neck is just 225km (140 miles) long.

Essential information:
Go west to east in the hope that a following wind pushes you over the Pennines. Then it's (mostly) downhill to Newcastle or Sunderland.

2

Ireland on foot

There are over 7000 pubs scattered across Ireland – and by the halfway point of your cross-country walk from Dublin to Portmagee on the Atlantic coast, you'll feel as though you've been inside most of them. Ireland is a country with a slower pace of life, so take your time on this 622km (386-mile) route, which stitches together waymarked trails through Wicklow, South Leinster, East Munster, Blackwater and Kerry. You'll feel pretty smug having completed six of the nation's long-distance paths when you settle in with a pint of Murphy's.

Essential information:
Recommended walking time for the whole route is 24 days.

3

Costa Rica on horseback

On each day of this sea-to-ocean odyssey you've faced totally new terrain with your Criollo steed, from soft Caribbean sand at the outset to the lushness of the Costa Rican rainforest. The highlands of this astonishingly diverse country will provide the main challenge, as you cross the back of Central America far away from the touristed path and descend to the Pacific coast. You'll pass through remote villages, Indigenous regions and protected parks.

Essential information:
The Camino de Costa Rica trail stretches for 280km (174 miles) and takes about 15 days to ride.

4

Australia's Savannah Way by 4WD

The epic Savannah Way skirts the top of Australia, and the section from Cairns to Broome is one of the country's great road trips. Leaving steamy Cairns and rising through rainforests to the Tablelands that tower above the Wet Tropics, a long, rough and remote road awaits. Driving in the hoofsteps of drovers, you'll negotiate 3700km (2300 miles) to reach Broome in the gorgeous Kimberley.

Essential information:
Visit during dry season. Roadhouses or service stations are often scarce; bring fuel canisters, spare tyres and drinking water.

Clockwise, from top: expect a rugged ride on Australia's Savannah Way; cross northern England's neck on a Sea to Sea cycle ride; conquer the Camino de Costa Rica on horseback

VACATION
MEETS VALUES

Tracey Minkin is on hand to replenish and regenerate in Mexico

Baby sea turtles are a gateway drug. You see, once you've witnessed these tablespoon-sized creatures hatch out of deep sandy nests dug by their mothers, make a brave, tiny-flippered dash down to the sea and begin a long solo swim to the relative safety of sargassum miles offshore, you choke back tears and vow to help them survive this arduous journey. To help every little sea turtle. To help all the sea turtles.

You're hooked. But what are you hooked on? Besieged by everything from motorboat strikes to ingestible plastics, a sea turtle's life is one of vulnerability at our own hands – humankind has officially endangered six of the world's seven species. So, you get hooked on a fierce form of reptile allyship, loving their strange, alien gazes, thrilling to videos of them swimming and, yes, crying at the sight of those tiny hatchlings racing towards uncertain futures amid predators, poachers and pollution.

But also, as I discovered after four eye-opening days in a remarkable little resort on Mexico's western coast, you can get hooked in a much bigger way, expanding your focus from a creature and outward to ocean, shore, jungle, farm, river, mountain – and how they all connect. You get hooked on feeling the pull of that web of life. And most importantly, you begin to see how your every choice tugs at those threads.

Is it any wonder that the founders of this place named it Playa Viva? The 'beach alive'?

I'd come here because a friend had shared the secret with me: here on a sleepy stretch of palm-studded beach, she said, was La Tortuga Viva, a fantastic grassroots program that passionately protects thousands of endangered sea turtles that return every year to nest on its beaches. 'But that was just the beginning,' she said.

'You had me at sea turtle,' I replied.

La Tortuga Viva was created by Playa Viva, a small Mexican resort that, for 15 years, had been quietly building a new way of hosting guests while regenerating the place it occupied. Here was a resort that worked to bring more life back to the world around it rather than draw from it. Yes, protecting the local turtle population. But also employing sustainable materials to create stunning lodgings that perched amid palms and were cooled by sea breezes. Using only the sun's energy to quietly electrify what needed it. Capturing, inventively treating and reusing its water and waste to sustain the resort's environs and support small-scale, regenerative farming on its 80 hectares (200 acres). And reaching beyond its borders into neighbouring communities, and up into the watershed in the Sierra Madre mountains to the east, to explore thoughtful ways to use the land and water better. This was not about plastic straws and not washing your towels every day (although there's nothing wrong with that). This was a quiet, beautiful revolution in what a hotel, a resort, could be.

I was on the next plane.

And there, to my delight, was the reclaimed-wood centre of La Tortuga Viva with its hand-painted sign, passionate local volunteers and pre-dawn patrols of the nesting grounds. Hatchlings that needed extra protection were carefully tended here until they could be released. Nests were minded.

But it was the rest of Playa Viva that set that bigger hook: a resort that sought thoughtfully, and worked hard, to make a beautiful place healthier than when it arrived. And what beauty! I slept in a treehouse with swooping lines inspired by migrating manta rays offshore, where bamboo latticework drew air around and through my room from every direction, all night long. With no air-conditioning on offer, the breath of the ocean became my own. I slept differently, deeper.

I slid into the Playa Viva rhythm, one of quiet and conversation. Meals were slow, organic and a crossroads of ideas: guests, staff, resident yogis and regenerative farming experts lingered at communal tables overlooking the sea.

And like the other lucky folks here, I spent unspooling time merely watching the shore – not for turtles by day,

as their work happened in the dark – but for the chevrons of pelicans skimming the barrel-waves offshore in search of fish. I felt the rivers descend from the mountains and nourish the ocean, the species feed and reproduce. I lost track of time and felt my surroundings take proper hold of me. I was, in every right way, hooked.

They say certain drugs can make you feel at one with the universe. I'd argue that chasing sea turtles to this corner of the world did the same. Do I still consider myself a sea-turtle stan, now and forever? You bet I do. But I also look around me now, in my post-Playa-Viva days, thinking daily of my food, my water, of what I do and how I consume, and of how I can build my own regenerative way in the world. And I thank those sweet sea turtles for leading me to that place.

HUNT A MONSTER

They seek him here! They seek him there! A land's social history is shaped by the people who have passed through over the centuries. With them come stories collected on their travels: tales of goblins and giants, fairy queens and woodland nymphs, devilish werewolves, unearthly phantoms, man-eating ogres and predatory ghouls. Some of these have morphed into what we now call cryptids – creatures whose very existence is based on human tales of sightings. Keep your eyes peeled.

1

Yeti
Himalaya

Of all ape-man legends, the Abominable Snowman is the most enduring and documented, perhaps because it occupies the remote foothills of Nepal and Tibet, leaving occasional footprints or stray hairs. At Tengboche Buddhist Monastery in Solukhumbu, older monks tell of a ferocious yeti attack on their yaks in the years before trekkers arrived. An important place of worship for Sherpas, Tengboche is the ideal place to start searching for a beast that's largely known from Sherpa tales.

Essential information:
Fly to Solukhumbu's
Tenzing-Hillary Airport
(also known as Lukla
Airport) from Kathmandu.

2

Nessie
Scotland

Deep, dark and narrow, Loch Ness stretches for 37km (23 miles) between Inverness and Fort Augustus. Its bitterly cold waters have been extensively explored in search of Nessie, the elusive monster first 'sighted' in 1933. Commanding a superb location just east of Drumnadrochit, with outstanding views (on a clear day), ruined Urquhart Castle is a Nessie-hunting hotspot. Its impressive five-storey tower-house remains, offering wonderful views across the loch.

Essential information:
A complete circuit of Loch
Ness is about 113km (70
miles) - go anticlockwise
for the better views.

3

Bunyip
Australia

In a land delineated by Aboriginal mythology, tales of the Bunyip are some of the more nightmarish. The beast – consistent descriptions are hard to find – inhabits swamps and rivers; when eerie screams are heard in the Outback at night, it's the Bunyip. Lurking in a cave on the Murray Bridge riverbank, a fabulously B-grade Bunyip statue has been terrifying kids since 1972. Press the button and a bald and bloodshot beast emerges, belching and rising from the water.

Essential information:
Murray Bridge, in South
Australia, sits 80km
(50 miles) from Adelaide.

4

Bigfoot
USA

Star of many a blurry Super-8 video, Bigfoot resides in the beautiful forests of the Pacific Northwest. It entered into popular folklore in the 1950s, when the region's wild woods were being explored by increasing numbers of hikers – but legends of Sasquatch are nothing new. Native American tribes passed down stories about large, hairy forest creatures, and settlers reported similar sightings as early as the 1800s.

Essential information:
Keep an eye out in Mt St Helena, Walla Walla and Bellingham, or head to the North American Bigfoot Center in Boring, Oregon.

Clockwise, from top: search for Nessie from Urquhart Castle; make yeti-hunting forays from Nepal's Tengboche Monastery; Bigfoot looming large in Willow Creek

HOUSE-SWAP SOMEWHERE SURPRISING

Get to know a neighbourhood over a week by swapping house keys with someone else (using one of several specialist apps). It's like a shortcut to being a local. It works best with less obvious locations: this is Santander, Spain.

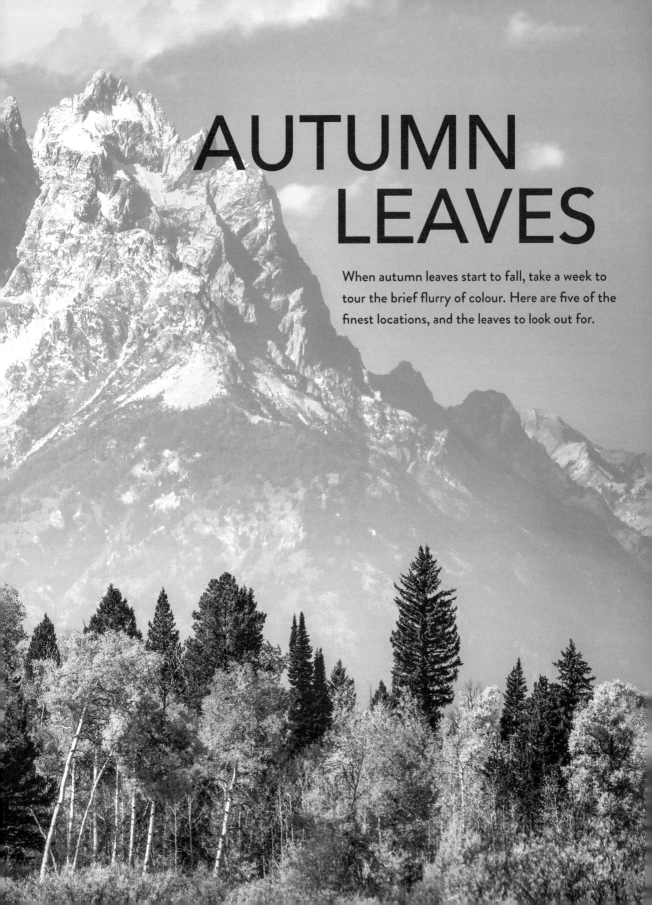

AUTUMN LEAVES

When autumn leaves start to fall, take a week to tour the brief flurry of colour. Here are five of the finest locations, and the leaves to look out for.

BEECH
FOREST OF DEAN, ENGLAND

This ancient woodland in Gloucestershire was once a royal hunting ground, and its trees were also used to make Tudor warships. Today, it's the perfect spot for the more prosaic sport of 'leaf peeping'. The mix of oak, beech and sweet chestnut provides a rusty riot of yellow and gold. Just keep an eye out for the wild boar that have called this place home since 2006.

MAPLE
NARA, JAPAN

Autumn in Japan is every bit as stunning as the short-lived *haname* (cherry blossom) season in spring. *Kouyou*, or autumn leaves, can be seen across the country, starting in the northern island of Hokkaidō and spreading quickly south from the end of September. The ancient capital of Nara, a short train ride from Kyoto, is a wonderful viewing spot. Its vast park is awash with colour, with sensational views of red, gold and yellow leaves along the paths up to Tamukeyama-hachimangū shrine in its northeast corner.

RED OAK
AGAWA CANYON, CANADA

Hop on board the Agawa Canyon Tour Train in autumn and you'll be treated to some of the planet's most beautiful fall foliage. The ride sets off from Sault Ste Marie on the Canada–USA border, covering 183km (114 miles) of unspoilt country that looks its best as the days begin to close in. The views here inspired Tom Thomson and the Group of Seven, Canada's most prominent landscape artists, throughout the early 20th century. You'll need to be quick, though, as the leaves peak for a brief period around the end of September and beginning of October.

ASH
WHITE MOUNTAINS, USA

New England is synonymous with fall and picking one must-see spot isn't easy. But New Hampshire's White Mountains are surely one of the best places – not just in New England, but in the whole world – to take in autumn at its most colourful. Hike through the hills at the start of October and you'll be treated to brilliant-red maple leaves. Or drive to Silver Cascade Falls in Carroll County to see the trees glow next to the 76m-high (250ft) waterfall.

ASPEN
COLORADO, USA

In Colorado, it's all about the aspen, a tree so ethereally beautiful they named a town and a beer after it. Over Kebler Pass, a gravel road out of Crested Butte that passes through Gunnison National Forest in southwest Colorado, the aspens glow golden in the autumn sun, the hills set afire with the quaking of a million leaves. September is the best month to visit: explore miles upon miles of trails under the bluebird Colorado sky.

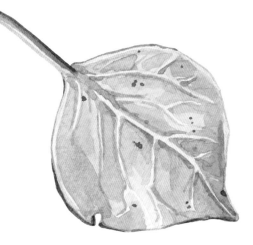

UNPLUG WITH TRADITIONAL HANDICRAFT

Realising the health benefits of handicrafts' meditative processes has been a true wellness revolution, breathing new life into pastimes once seen as the preserve of bygone eras. From textile crafts like knitting, crochet, macramé and embroidery to pottery, woodcraft and weaving, the modern iterations of these ancient techniques are not only beneficial for anyone looking for a mindful escape – they can also offer uniquely intimate ways to explore the cultures into which they are woven.

1

Macramé
Lambay Island, Ireland

Nestled within the folds of the Irish Sea, Lambay is a nurturing and nourishing environment in which to get to grips with the ancient art of macramé, newly popular as a boho interior design feature: macramé wall hangings and pot holders feature on countless Pinterest boards and Instagram feeds. Running over a long weekend, Lambay's macramé retreat combines the contemplative process of learning to knot with restorative yoga classes, all in the island's dramatically beautiful surrounds.

Essential information:
Retreats on Lambay typically take place in spring, and start from around €540 per person for three days.

Far left to right: working the wool for weaving in Oaxaca, Mexico; intricate patterns on Icelandic knits; refine your knitting skills amid Iceland's dramatic landscapes

2

Weaving & dyeing
Oaxaca, Mexico

Guided by a skilled community of weavers and natural dyers in the vibrant city of Oaxaca, you can gradually learn these deeply absorbing arts using a traditional floor loom and dyes made from locally sourced plants and pigments. The slow but rewarding method of weaving is perfect for mentally checking out from the daily grind, and connecting to an ancient art that has been a part of Oaxacan culture for centuries – taught by those who know it best.

Essential information:
Oaxaca weaving retreats with Thread Caravan take place throughout the year, and start from around $2900 per person for seven days.

3

Woodwork
Alaskan wilderness, USA

If spending a week learning to carve, whittle and woodwork among enchanting Alaskan boreal forest sounds like the kind of back-to-nature restoration you crave, head to the Folk School in Fairbanks. Their 'Week in the Woods' retreat promotes the healing power of woodlands via skill-sharing and workshops, and focuses on advocating for environmental stewardship and sustainable forestry techniques, aiming to deepen our affinity with the natural world.

Essential information:
The Folk School's six-day 'Week in the Woods' retreats take place year-round, and start from around $900 per person for six days.

4

Knitting in the wilds
Iceland

As fortification against the country's naturally unforgiving climate, traditional Icelandic knitting produces intricate designs that are equal parts visually mesmerising and practically insulating. Retreats with Icelandic Knitter combine learning traditional techniques with absorbing the sweeping landscapes and captivating local folklore that Iceland is known for. Locations range from the breathtaking Westfjords to the mystical 'peninsular of the trolls'.

Essential information:
Retreats with Icelandic Knitter take place throughout the year, and start from around €1650 per person for six/seven days.

"MANY STORIES
HAVE BEEN USED TO
MALIGN. BUT STORIES
TO EMPOWER
STORIES CAN BREAK
PEOPLE. BUT STORIES
THAT BROKEN

MATTER. STORIES
DISPOSSESS AND TO
CAN ALSO BE USED
AND TO HUMANIZE.
THE DIGNITY OF A
CAN ALSO REPAIR
DIGNITY."

– CHIMAMANDA ADICHIE

ISLANDS OF ADVENTURE

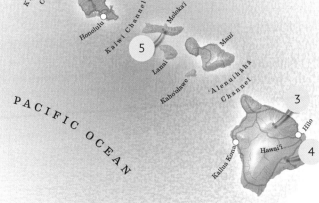

Get there
The Hawaiʻian archipelago is in the Pacific Ocean. The main airport is Honolulu. There are frequent flights between islands.

A WEEK IN HAWAIʻI, USA

Forget escaping to an island to kick back and drift off: these islands are designed for an action-packed week of escapades through mountains, jungles and volcanoes.

1
Oʻahu, North Shore
North Shore surfing is not for the novice or the fainthearted; giant swells slam into Oʻahu from the deep ocean. But as a place to see masters of their craft at work, it is unequalled.

2
Nā Pali Coast, Kauaʻi
Sea kayaks are the best way to access the Nā Pali Coast Wilderness Park; paddling in is permitted from May to September, though it's not an excursion for beginners.

3
Mauna Kea, Big Island
Stargaze at the Onizuka Center for International Astronomy on top of the dormant volcano of Mauna Kea. Telescopes are available until 10pm.

4
Kīlauea, Big Island
Hike in the Hawaiʻi Volcanoes National Park; the Crater Rim Trail around the edge of Kīlauea, a dormant voclano, features rainforest, desert and volcanic vents.

5
Molokaʻi Island
Chill out on Molokaʻi, the low-key island that's home to Hawaiʻi's largest population of Native people, and has no high-rise resorts. Take jungle drives or tropical forest walks.

1

Sa Gubia
Rock-climb at this huge rock amphitheatre west of Bunyola. It's Mallorca's top sport-climbing spot and the Spanish limestone is superb.

2

Söller
Cycle north or south from Söller into the heart of the Tramuntana range for some of Europe's best bike-riding routes. It's easy to put together loops though the mountains; spring and autumn are the prime seasons.

3

Santa Ponsa
Sail out of the smart and sheltered harbour of Santa Ponsa to join one of Europe's most popular yachting scenes. Charters and courses are available.

4

Parc Natural de Mondragó
Close to Santanyí, kick back on the park's secluded beaches after your exertions; all are accessed via short hikes down stony paths.

5

Parc Natural de s'Albufera
Birdwatch at these wetlands on the north coast, with more than 200 species – residents and visitors – to spot. Bring your binoculars!

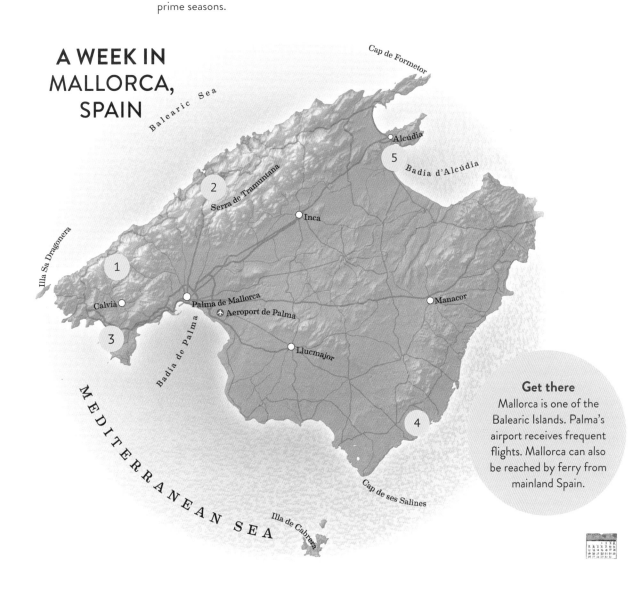

A WEEK IN MALLORCA, SPAIN

Balearic Sea

Cap de Formetor

Alcúdia

5

Badia d'Alcúdia

2

Serra de Tramuntana

Inca

Illa Sa Dragonera

1

Calvià

Palma de Mallorca

Aeroport de Palma

Manacor

Badia de Palma

3

Llucmajor

MEDITERRANEAN SEA

4

Get there
Mallorca is one of the Balearic Islands. Palma's airport receives frequent flights. Mallorca can also be reached by ferry from mainland Spain.

Cap de ses Salines

Illa de Cabrera

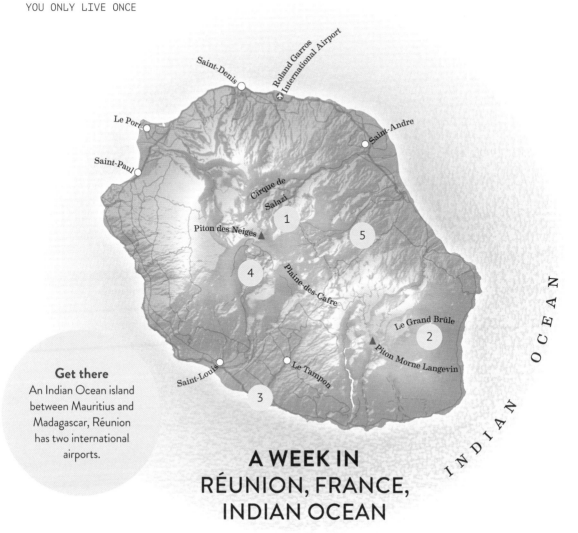

Saint-Denis

Roland Garros
International Airport

Le Port

Saint-Andre

Saint-Paul

Cirque de
Salazi

1

5

Piton des Neiges ▲

4

Plaine-des-Cafre

Le Grand Brûle

2

Piton Morne Langevin ▲

Saint-Louis

Le Tampon

3

INDIAN OCEAN

Get there
An Indian Ocean island
between Mauritius and
Madagascar, Réunion
has two international
airports.

A WEEK IN
RÉUNION, FRANCE,
INDIAN OCEAN

1	**2**	**3**	**4**	**5**
Hell-Bourg	**Piton de la Fournaise**	**St Pierre**	**Cirque de Cilaos**	**Grand Étang**
Savour a cold beer in a rural bar among Creole musicians in this pretty village amid the island's verdant interior.	Climb this active volcano if it's not too lively. The five-hour trek up the loose, sun-scorched slopes is challenging, but the view down into the crater and across the Indian Ocean is worth the effort.	Party in Réunion's third-largest town, in the island's southwest, which pulses with a hedonistic energy after dark.	Hike in the spectacular setting of a steep, volcanic crest. There's a variety of canyoning trips in these snaggle-toothed peaks where you'll be climbing, abseiling and simply sliding down the slopes.	Riding a horse around the largest lake on Réunion is a low-impact way to soak up the drop-dead gorgeous scenery. Horseback trips into the interior can last a few hours or several days.

1

Whitehaven Beach, Whitsunday Island

Beachcomb amid talcum-powder-fine sand on one of the world's most fabulous beaches.

2

Blue Pearl Bay, Hayman Island

Scuba dive at Hayman Island, one of the 74 islands in the Whitsunday archipelago and a top diving destination.

3

Proserpine River, Queensland

Spot saltwater crocs – and other Aussie critters – in these estuaries on a crocodile safari departing from Airlie Beach.

4

Airlie Beach, Queensland

Learn to sail a yacht or begin a bareboating trip at Airlie's Whitsunday Sailing Club – sailing is the heart and soul of the Whitsundays.

5

Shute Harbour, Queensland

Set out in sea kayaks from Shute Harbour and paddle bay to bay through glassy waters, watching out for whales, dolphins and turtles.

A WEEK IN QUEENSLAND & THE WHITSUNDAYS, AUSTRALIA

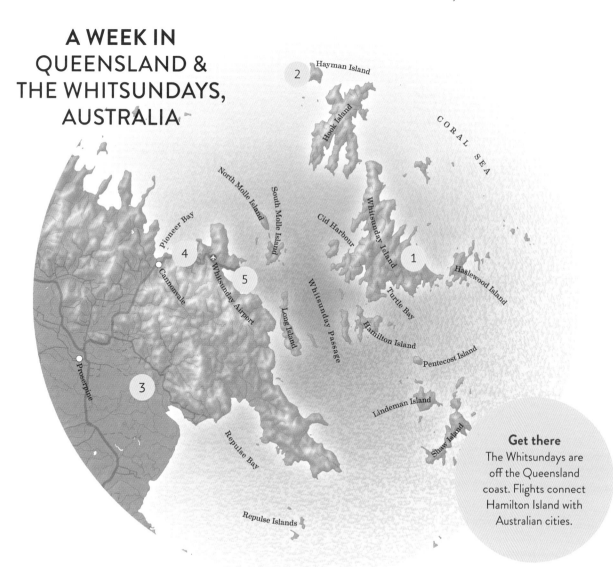

Get there
The Whitsundays are off the Queensland coast. Flights connect Hamilton Island with Australian cities.

TREKKING A RAINFOREST

Shafik Meghji explores one of the Earth's last surviving wildernesses.

As an inky darkness descended on the rainforest, I carefully picked my way through a clearing dotted with lime and pomelo trees to the edge of Laguna Chalalán. My guide, William – a member of the Indigenous Quechua-Tacana community of San José de Uchupiamonas – was waiting in a wooden canoe. After paddling out to the centre of the lake, deep inside Parque Nacional Madidi, we took it in turns to scan our torches along the shoreline, periodically catching the eye of a caiman which flashed crimson-red in the light. Half a metre (2ft) long, with thin, gangly bodies, the reptiles gazed back warily before vanishing below the surface.

'They're just babies,' said William. 'The adults can grow to twice that size.' Yikes.

Nothing quite prepares you for being in the Amazon, one of the world's last surviving wildernesses. I was drawn to Madidi, in northwestern Bolivia, because of its sheer abundance of life. In 2018, the Wildlife Conservation Society declared it 'the world's most biologically diverse protected area', home to more than 8800 species, many of which are endemic.

William and I switched off our torches and sat in comfortable silence, transfixed by the countless stars on a jet-black canvas, as a chorus of croaking frogs, clicking bats and humming cicadas drifted across the water.

Having spent just a few days in the reserve, it felt like I'd seen all 8800 species, such is the profusion of mammals, birds, reptiles, fish, insects, plants and trees everywhere you look. But where Madidi overdelivered in its biodiversity, it provided me with a stark reminder of the precariousness of the Amazon.

My journey began in the far-flung town of Rurrenabaque, a hot and humid former rubber-trading post that has become a hub for ecotourism in recent decades. On the waterfront I met William for a boat journey along the serpentine, chocolate-brown Beni and Tuichi rivers, which wind through the Madidi reserve. After navigating a narrow, mist-shrouded gorge, the rocky cliffs flattened out, the hills beyond them slowly disappeared from view and thick walls of foliage rose along the banks.

I watched storks and woodpeckers dart overhead, while multicoloured dragonflies and butterflies buzzed and skimmed across the water. Deftly navigating rapids, sandbanks and clumps of floating branches, William told me about some of the other species found in Madidi's rainforests, cloudforests, grasslands and wetlands.

'There are pink dolphins known as *bufeos*, jaguars, anacondas, stingrays, birds of paradise, spectacled bears, macaws, capybaras and many, many others.'

But the journey also highlighted threats. We passed the site of proposed hydroelectric dams that could well flood a vast region; encountered a pair of gold miners working away on a stony beach; spotted patches of deforestation from encroaching farmers, ranchers and loggers, whose activities are also linked to devastating wildfires.

Five hours after setting off from Rurrenabaque we arrived at the Chalalán Ecolodge, which was founded by the people of San José de Uchupiamonas to provide local jobs, fund development projects and promote sustainable tourism. Following that evening of caiman-spotting and stargazing on the lagoon, I sat with William on the terrace, swapping stories as the rainforest gradually quietened down for the night.

The next morning we hiked to the Santa Rosa Lake, William expertly wielding a machete, in a manner I could only dream of emulating, to cut a path through the dense undergrowth that swiftly enveloped us. There was sound and movement all around me: tapirs – cow-sized mammals with elephantine snouts – charged through the undergrowth, while troupes of squirrel, capuchin and howler monkeys crashed about in the canopy, competing for the choicest leaves. Every branch and tree trunk was a miniature world, draped in shaggy epiphytes and patrolled by fire ants, tiny lizards and tarantulas at least the size of my hand.

As the rainforest echoed with the songs and alarm calls of parrots, macaws, spiky-crested hoatzins and red-breasted trogons, William pointed out fresh jaguar tracks in the mud and showed me the fantastical walking palm, whose stilt-like roots allow it to move, at a glacial pace, across the forest floor in search of sunlight and favourable soils. We reached the Santa Rosa Lake, a turquoise mirror fringed by overhanging trees, and I spent the afternoon fishing for piranhas before stumbling upon a family of peccaries, wild-boar-like creatures that emit high-pitched squeals.

We made it back to the lodge just before nightfall. Muddy, sweaty and parched, I guzzled glass after glass of sugared lime juice before launching myself into the lagoon to cool off, keeping a careful eye out for any caimans that might be lurking in the vicinity. As I swam – or, more accurately, nervously splashed about – I tried to tot up the number of birds and animals I'd seen before quickly losing count.

In that moment Madidi felt vast and timeless. Humbling and awe-inspiring. But, more than anything, I was left with a heightened awareness of the challenges facing the Amazon – and of our responsibility to protect it.

LONG-DISTANCE HIKING

Humans have long been walking for health, pleasure, problem-solving and connection with the land and each other. Science has proven what we knew instinctively: walking sets thoughts free and brings people together; it's good for the brain, body and community. And our feet can carry us where cars can't. So, take the scenic route with a long-distance hike, and you'll likely discover a clearer mind and killer views – not to mention new friends – along the way.

1

Trans Bhutan Trail
Bhutan
Follow in the footsteps of monks, traders and royals in one of the globe's happiest and greenest countries (tree-filled Bhutan absorbs more carbon than it produces). This cross-country trail linking ancient pilgrimage and communications routes takes in mountain passes, forested valleys, heritage sites and rural villages. Exchange stories and meals with residents in this spiritually and culturally rich place: this is more than a hike – it's a journey for the soul.

Essential information:
Choose a section, or trek the full 403km (250-mile) length of the trail in a month. Paro is Bhutan's only international airport.

2

Jordan Trail
Jordan
Wander the world and you'll never find a trail like this, starting among olive trees and Greco-Roman ruins, finishing at the Red Sea, and with multiple Unesco-listed sites en route – including the rock-carved city of Petra and the Mars-like landscapes of Wadi Rum. Built along Bedouin footpaths, the Jordan Trail also heads off the tourist track to places inaccessible by car: slow down and embrace the desert's beauty and challenging extremes.

Essential information:
Choose a section or trek the full 675km (419 miles) over several weeks. Arrive via Queen Alia (Amman) or King Hussein (Aqaba) airports.

3

wukalina Walk
Tasmania, Australia
This shorter but more accessible trail is the only multi-day hike on the planet led by palawa (Tasmania's Indigenous people). Everything here – the ribbons of kelp, the tunnels of eucalyptus trees, the tiniest of seashells (and yes, wombats, wallabies and other wildlife) – vibrates with stories of palawa who walked before you. Sink your toes in the sand and watch the sunset atop Mt William as your guide reveals connections between the past, the land, palawa – and you.

Essential information:
Meet your guides in Launceston. Direct flights are available to Launceston Airport from several major cities in Australia.

4

Transcaucasian Trail
Multi-country

Get way – way – off the beaten path in one of Europe's most culturally diverse regions. Intrepid, self-sufficient hikers can become part of history by tackling the Transcaucasian (TCT), a growing network of trails (covering 3000km/1864 miles in total) that cross the Caucasus Mountains, multiple countries and over 20 national parks and protected areas – plus ancient monasteries, wineries, alpine meadows and more.

Essential information:
```
TCT hikes in Armenia,
Georgia and Azerbaijan range
from four to 10 days; or be
one of the first to thru-hike
Armenia (25-45 days).
```

Clockwise, from top: make a spiritual pilgrimage on the Trans Bhutan Trail; wander with wallabies on the wukalina Walk; follow Bedouin byways on the Jordan Trail

CHAPTER 4

A MONTH

UNDER A
CITY'S SKIN

Rather than see as many places as you can
in a short time, why not spend as long as you
can in one place and really get to know it? A
month in a city like Athens, Greece will help
you get under its skin and discover more than
the Acropolis.

THE ART OF PLAY

It's not just for kids. Seriously. Studies show that play is crucial, no matter what your age. But what exactly is 'play'? Psychiatrist Dr Stuart Brown, founder of the National Institute for Play (yes, this exists!) defines play as a 'state of mind that one has when absorbed in an activity that provides enjoyment and a suspension of sense of time.' This could be almost anything, from sports to board games to dancing to noodling on the guitar. Benefits include greater mental sharpness, social wellbeing and physical health.

1

Noosa Heads
Australia

Anyone with a bucket can build a sandcastle, but how about a 3m-high (10ft) sand dragon breathing sculpted fire? Take your sand-building skills up a notch – or ten – with a sandcastle workshop in the Queensland beach town of Noosa Heads. A master sandcastle-builder will show you how to create life-size sand mermaids, Gaudí-like surrealist towers or whatever else your imagination desires. It'll only last until the tide comes in but, of course, the impermanence is part of the fun.

Essential information: Sandshapers offers 1hr 30min workshops at Noosa's Sunshine Beach, about a 2hr drive north of Brisbane.

2

Pennsylvania
USA

The braces may be off your teeth, but you're not too old for the beloved American tradition of summer camp. At grownups-only Camp No Counselors, adulting is ditched in favour of dodgeball, arts and crafts, archery, paintball, kayaking and roasting s'mores. And unlike kid camp, this version comes with an open bar. There's no lights-out time, so feel free to stargaze and singalong until the wee hours before retreating to your bunk. Don't forget to prepare something for the talent show – there will be prizes!

Essential information: Camp No Counselors has several US locations, including this one, a 3hr drive northwest of New York City.

3

Buñol
Spain

Imagine the world's biggest food fight, with no teachers screaming at you to 'stop or your parents will hear about this!' Each August, Spain's La Tomatina festival brings thousands together to hurl tomatoes at each other for literally no reason besides fun. Swimsuit-clad revellers run through the streets covered in red pulp, dodging tomato bombs and yelping in delight. When it's all done, the fire department hoses everyone and everything off, and the party heads to the local swimming pool.

Essential information: La Tomatina is the last Wednesday in August in Buñol, 1hr west of Valencia by train.

4

Essen
Germany

Since 1983, this town in northwest Germany has hosted Essen SPIEL, the biggest board game fair in the world. Fans gather for the newest and greatest in strategy, adventure, card, fantasy and computer games. Chat with game designers, sit down at booths to try new games, join a chess competition, don chain mail and dodge dragons in a medieval LARP (live action role-playing game), or play cards late into the night at the convention hotel bar. Play is a serious business here.

Essential information: Essen is in northwest Germany, 30min by train from Dusseldorf, 2hr from Frankfurt and 3hr from Amsterdam.

Far left to right: take sandcastles to another level at Noosa Heads; top-to-toe tomatoes at Spain's La Tomatina; head to Essen, Germany, for the ultimate gamers' expo

MAKE PLANS WITHOUT PLANES

Dan Fahey forgoes flying in favour of travelling by land and sea.

Do I want to play dice for some Communist Party cigarettes?

Yeah, why not. I've only got 72 near-sleepless hours in China – a warp-speed, deep-end, whistlestop swing around the country's southernmost point, Hainan Island – so I'm up for trying anything. As long as it's quick.

I've already been under the neon bulbs of Haikou's night market for a while, its pop music booming out louder than an explosion at a Hawai'ian shirt factory. I've lined my stomach with grilled duck throat, which was so spicy that it razed my taste buds like an atomic bomb. Yesterday, I surfed for the first time, riding sapphire-green waves at honeycomb-coloured Riyue Bay on the southeast of the island. This is what I love about travel: trying new things and essentially getting stuck in.

But back to the dice. Even if I were to lose to the two beer-razzled locals, Tony and Mr Do, who had staggered over to my table to invite me to play, would I really be losing at all? These encounters don't happen nearly enough, so I agree to play.

They pull up a red plastic stool each and get the beers in – a 3L (5-pint) lager fountain that sweats under the sticky heat of the evening. It comes with complementary roasted peanuts and a plate of soft-shell crabs, smothered in chunky fried onions and a generous sprinkling of garlic. Game on.

For the most part, this was how I used to travel. Find a flight, pack little more than a passport and my pants, and zip off somewhere, taking in as much as I could in as little time as possible. A long weekend in China from London? Sure. Porto for a couple of nights? Book it.

But then, in late 2018, I was sitting in an airport lounge when something leapt out of whatever dull business newspaper I was reading that changed my travel plans forever: The Graph. I looked at it and instantly went hot with fear.

I put down the paper and pushed away my croissant. I scoped around, trying to catch someone's attention. But no one seemed bothered. They clearly hadn't heard the news, hence why they were acting as usual: studying departure boards or dashing off with their rolling suitcases.

Surely they must know? The work of Harvard galaxy-brains, the line chart plotted the Earth's average global temperatures over the last 11 millennia. It showed the mercury rising and falling incrementally across thousands of years until around 1900, when it suddenly shot up vertically, going beyond the levels which had previously taken 6000 years in the last century alone.

In short: we were screwed. The planet was heating up like a furnace and we were chucking more coal into the flames. So what was I to do? Stride onto the plane, bury my head in an in-flight movie and try to and forget about the whole thing? I had to give up flying.

It was one of the best decisions I've ever made.

Travelling without an aeroplane was like learning to walk again. Since going cold turkey, I travel at a more harmonious pace with the planet. I'm more in tune with my surroundings.

On a slow narrowboat trip north along England's Grand Union Canal, I could see the day unfold in all of its slow-wound glory: dawn joggers running along the towpath and horses galloping through shaggy green fields by the time the kettle whistled.

In India, travelling by train was possibly the ultimate experience. We clambered aboard a slow-moving carriage at Varanasi, and shared meals of dal, steamed rice and pickles, all mopped up by a chapati, with our Indian carriage-mate Raj, a local doctor who invited us into his home to meet his family.

I made friends during a 36-hour bus journey between Luang Prabang, quiet former royal capital of Laos, and the hectic, watch-your-step buzz of Hanoi in Vietnam. We bonded over *bánh tét* (sticky rice and mung-bean cakes, steamed and served in a banana leaf) and went for beers once we pulled into town.

For me, these overland journeys and short-lived interactions are the soul of travelling. This is where the action happens. It's where to embed myself, and it's much better for the planet and my psyche.

Truth be told, slow travel is better than the grab-and-go trips I used to take, too. I did win a packet of those special Communist Party cigarettes playing dice with Tony and Mr Do. We shared a ceremonious smoke together. I toasted my success by searing my lungs.

The pair wanted to play some more and I wanted to stay drinking, but I had to leave. I had to get back to my hotel, grab my bag, and head to the airport for my flight back to Beijing. I'd reached the fag-end of the trip too quickly. But if I ever return without flying, I'm up for another round. And I won't be in a rush to leave.

"A CHILD CAN
THREE THINGS: TO
NO REASON, TO
WITH SOMETHING,
HOW TO DEMAND
MIGHT THAT

TEACH AN ADULT BE HAPPY FOR ALWAYS BE BUSY AND TO KNOW WITH ALL HIS WHICH HE DESIRES."

– PAULO COELHO

CIRCUMNAVIGATING THE WORLD

Holly Tuppen takes a round-the-world trip by bike, boat and bus.

At 2am, somewhere in the middle of the Atlantic, a teeth-clenching crack and a thud broke the calming monotony of the wind in the sails and water swooshing past the hull. At 1600 nautical miles from land, disaster struck our seafaring home – a sturdy 15m (50ft) Norwegian ketch (a 1930s fishing boat) with proud red sails and rickety bunks. Five of us, strangers united by a need to get across the Atlantic without flying, flew out of beds cursing, panicking and jumping into action. Our main mast had snapped in half, pulling down sails and now hanging precariously over the side of the boat. Radios crackled, the lifeboat was prepped and an angle-grinder threw sparks into the night sky, cutting the mass of wood and sails free so we wouldn't capsize.

Just as dawn hinted its arrival, tinting the never-ending midnight blue with a welcome golden glow, the monotony of wind in the sails and water on the hull returned. We were back on our way, half a sail down and going at half the speed – but safe. After 31 days at sea, we sailed into the balmy turquoise waters of Sint-Maarten, a tiny island in the north of the Caribbean's Leeward Islands. Turtles bobbed nonchalantly around the boat, noisy bars lined the harbour beach and a cruise ship towered overhead. Land comforts beckoned, but first we paused in our salt-crusted bubble, glugging back rum to celebrate successfully crossing an ocean using nothing but the power of the wind.

Two years earlier, I'd barely set foot on a sailing boat. Nor had I ridden a tandem bike, hitchhiked, wild-camped

or followed dusty pilgrim routes across entire countries. That all changed the day my partner and I, jaded with London life, bought a giant world map, scribbled adventure aspirations all over it, and squirrelled away whatever cash we could.

Plans grew more and more elaborate, and we soon decided to turn a fun adventure into an epic one by not flying. Why not cycle up the US? How about sailing the Atlantic? Isn't there a walking route across Spain? Did I read about hopping on container ships across the Pacific? We had a hunch that in a world that can't stop speeding up, the greatest luxury would be to slow it right down.

Telling everyone we knew meant we couldn't back out, and soon, one drizzly Sunday in September, loved ones gathered in Hyde Park to wave us off on a heavily loaded secondhand tandem. Twenty months, 83,680km (52,000 miles), 15 modes of transport and 31 countries later, we cycled back into Hyde Park. We'd lost a stone each, stank, and London was still drizzly.

Along the way, we'd experienced things no brochure or Instagram feed could have prepared us for. Some ideas went to plan, like sailing the Atlantic, jumping on a container ship from Vancouver to South Korea, and cycling the tandem across Europe and the US. But challenges were thrown our way, too. In Central America, we had to shelter from gun violence one night. In China, we were relentlessly followed and moved on by the police. On the western coast of Canada, we bit off more than we could chew on a kayak expedition from which we were lucky to return.

Plans also shifted. We worked in Nepal for four months to save money rather than travel around Southeast Asia and, due to the snapped mast, we had to beg our way on to boats of every shape and size to get from one end of the Caribbean to the other. We almost packed the whole trip in after a nasty bike accident in Istanbul. The standout memories, however, were spellbinding moments with people and nature, whether cycling past grizzly bears in Yellowstone, being followed by a minke whale across the Atlantic, or the privilege of being welcomed into people's homes and seeing a snapshot of their lives from the Himalaya to Hungary.

Most of us know the environmental benefits of ditching flights and going overland, but the joy of slow travel doesn't stop there. Drifting through countries and across borders without leaving the ground forced us to relinquish control and embrace the unknown. We often couldn't choose where we went, or things didn't pan out as we'd expected. But it's in these moments that real life unfurls in all its complex magic: crammed into a jeep across the Taklamakan Desert; sari-shopping for a Nepali wedding; stranded on a broken-down bus in Colombia; wearing socks for gloves during a surprise blizzard in Colorado; bowled over by kindness in places that tourists are usually told to avoid. Going slow brought a vulnerability and openness to our journey that seemed to make the world smile at us – a life-affirming antidote to the negative and divisive commentary we so often hear. Hopefully, it's something that will stick with us for years to come.

CABIN IN THE WOODS

We all need a little breathing space. Head deep into the woods or the mountains to stay in a rustic retreat of your own. Few people can have read Henry David Thoreau's *Walden* and not dreamed of staying the night in a timber-walled bolthole in a sunlit glade, somewhere far from the asphalt world. From stone shepherds' huts to remote mountain bothies, there's no better refuge after a day well spent in the wilderness.

1

Friggebod
Sweden

If you're looking to create a traditional Scandi hideaway cabin deep in the woods, you're in luck. Since 1979, Sweden's building code has permitted the construction of buildings of less than 8 sq metres (90 sq ft) without a permit. These bijoux boxes, called *friggebod*, are typically found on family-owned plots in the wilds, overlooking lakes. The term derives from the name of a former Swedish housing minister, Birgit Friggebo, who helped scrap the need for a permit to build one.

Essential information:
Some *friggebod* are available to rent, but you're better off calling on any Swedish connections you may have.

Far left to right: find pint-sized perfection in a Swedish *friggebod*; follow in the footsteps of shepherds to a Pyrenean *orri*; Scotland's bothies range from frugal to fancy

2

Bach
New Zealand

You don't have to go far in New Zealand to escape the crowds: after WWII, holiday houses started popping up in scenic locations across the nation. The traditional, small Kiwi holiday home, known as a 'bach' (pronounced 'batch', and a diminutive of 'bachelor'), is often near a favourite (secret) beach, lake, forest or trout-fishing river. Many have a hand-built, hand-me-down look, but agencies have plenty of modern baches available to rent.

Essential information:
Most baches can be found on New Zealand's North Island – some are known as 'cribs' in the South Island.

3

Shepherd's hut
France & Spain

Traditional shepherds in the Pyrenees didn't have an easy job, spending weeks alone in the mountains, warding off bears and wolves. But when the weather turned nasty they had cosy stone refuges to retreat into. Known as an *orri* in the eastern Pyrenees, these stone igloos were built by hand, and often without mortar. Though it's rare to find a hut in which you can stand upright in, many still offer shelter to hikers who venture off the beaten track.

Essential information:
You'll find a smattering of orri in Ariège; main sites include Auzat, Vicdessos and the valley of Soulcem.

4

Bothy
Scotland, UK

Pull on your hiking boots and grab your Gore-Tex to seek out the Scottish interpretation of a mountain hut – the bothy. The Mountain Bothies Association (MBA) maintains around 100 shelters, most of them old cottages, in the most popular parts of the Highlands, but there are many more located in less frequented glens, which are often carefully guarded secrets. As the MBA says, you need to be proficient in using a map and compass to find them.

Essential information:
Find bothies via regions on the MBA website. Most lie a good few hours from public roads.

FOLLOW IN FAMOUS FEMALE FOOTSTEPS

Some say that behind every great man is a great woman. But great women have not only supported – and often been the brains behind and alongside – many successful men, they've also long been carving out their own paths as innovators, athletes, activists, academics, philanthropists and more, even if history has not always recognised them. Travel to the places where trailblazing women have worked, ruled, wandered and won Olympic gold, and you'll find incredible landscapes, challenging adventures and historic sites, as well as inspiration from the powerful women who walked here before you.

1

Luxor
Egypt

Hatshepsut was one of the few – and most successful – women to rule Egypt as a pharaoh. Her two-decade reign was characterised by peace and prosperity, and though her successors obliterated carvings commemorating her, her mark on history remains – as does the Mortuary Temple of Hatshepsut. It's in Luxor, a Nile Valley treasure-trove of ancient temples and monuments that's considered one of the world's largest open-air museums.

Essential information:
From Cairo, you can reach Luxor via a 1hr flight, an 11hr train or bus ride, or a multi-day Nile cruise.

2

Mount Everest
Nepal

Very few have summited all 14 'eight-thousanders' (peaks over 8000m/26,647ft) without sherpas and supplementary oxygen; Austrian Gerlinde Kaltenbrunner became the first woman to join this elite club in 2011. You don't have to summit 14 peaks unsupported – or even one – to experience their beauty and a sense of achievement: get a taste of high-altitude life on the 130km (81-mile) roundtrip trek to Everest Base Camp, at 5300m (17,600ft).

Essential information:
Hikes to Everest Base Camp start in Khumbu, Nepal, and can typically be completed in 12 days.

3

Sydney
Australia

At the Sydney 2000 Olympics, Cathy Freeman lit the cauldron and went on to win gold for the 400m sprint, making history as the first Australian Aboriginal individual to win gold and to carry both the Australian and Aboriginal flags on her victory lap. In 2007 she established the Cathy Freeman Foundation to support Indigenous education. Check out the Olympic cauldron at Cathy Freeman Park, then see the rest of Australia with Indigenous guides.

Essential information:
Indigenous-led urban tours, outback safaris and arts and cultural activities are available in all six states and in two territories.

4

Route of Parks
Chile

In 2019, on behalf of her late husband Doug and Tompkins Conservation, Kristine Tompkins made the largest privately held land donation in history, transferring Pumalín Douglas Tompkins and Patagonia national parks – over 4046 sq km (1562 sq miles) – to the Chilean government, who added another 36,000 sq km (13,900 sq miles) of federal land. The result? Patagonia holds 85% of Chile's protected lands, pristine and open to all.

Essential information: Access the glaciers, fjords and volcanoes of these spectacular national parks via Chile's Route of Parks.

Clockwise, from top: Chile's Pumalín Douglas Tompkins National Park; Cathy Freeman after winning Olympic gold in 2000; Mortuary Temple of Hatshepsut, Luxor

TAKE A LONG HIKE

A growing number of long-distance hiking trails demand a month or more of putting one foot in front of another, such as the new Jordan Trail. You'll discover hidden resources of resilience that you didn't realise you possessed. And a new-found appreciation of broken-in hiking boots.

SEEK OUT SECRET PLACES

Ben Handicott crosses the language barrier in China.

It's New Year's Eve, and I'm in a regional city in China. The roads are busy with cars the way department stores are with people during the sales. There's little movement, though, just a great deal of noise. I shuffle along the street, a path of neon and people – so many people. Amid the throng, I move as a tide, inevitable and unstoppable. Vendors selling balloons or steamed buns push through, attracting the hungry and annoying the many.

In two hours of shunting along like this, I don't say a word. And I don't understand a word. Everyone is intent on making their way to wherever. No one gives me a second look. Words fly meaninglessly around me; banners and signs are majestically unreadable. Everything is more or less familiar – people, streets, business, eating, laughter – but the overwhelming sense of confusion, of exclusion, leaves me with no touchstone at all. There's a mild sense of panic. I can't ask anybody a question. I can't read anything except the occasional brand-name on a billboard. I haven't learned the language and I'm unable to speak to anyone.

The crowd stirs; something has been communicated. There's a lull and people stop moving. Then a flash and, as I look up, a clap like thunder. A booming salvo of fireworks. A noise of equal strength rises from the city as people cheer, then the fireworks retort. Clouds of smoke grow and

confetti drifts above me. An hour of strobing light: gold, red and green lacework against the night, and the constant barrage of explosions – it's numbing. And then it stops and the elation of the crowd turns to fatigue. Beneath the orange glow of streetlights, through the filtering smoke, colour is leached from the banners and neon signs; all the brightness turn to sepia and as the crowds disperse, I head back the way I came, and no one says a word.

Can I recall being unable to speak my own language when I was little? When words spoken were just noises, tones of approval (or not); written language just scribbles? Imagine that feeling. Helpless, maybe; but unconcerned – surely.

Would it hurt to really tune out, to rediscover a sense of unconcern? Travel can give you this gift.

If you find yourself in a country that doesn't speak the language – or languages – that you do, and you are struggling to learn the lingo, give it a go. Stay away from the main cities. You won't need to travel far – an hour from the capital will do it. Then just… wander.

Go as far as you can from your base. Catch a bus. Stumble through transactions. Smile. Learn other ways in which to communicate. You might only live once but you can be a child again in a flash.

GO END-TO-END

Starting from one corner of a country and making your way to the opposite guarantees mental, physical and cartographic satisfaction. The most interesting top-to-toe journeys wind through a nation unconventionally, stringing together national trails, public footpaths or oceanside roads. As you near that final sign that announces your end-of-the-road, you are spent, yet have never felt more alive. You remember that quote – was it TS Eliot? Buddha? Bob Marley? – 'it's not the arrival that matters, but the joy of the journey'.

1

Ho Chi Minh Trail
Vietnam

Vietnam's twin megacities – Hanoi and Ho Chi Minh City – are divided by 1137km (707 miles) of mountains, jungles, paddy fields, beaches and historic sites: perfect country for road tripping. The Ho Chi Minh Trail, used to distribute Viet Cong supplies, has been named 'one of the great achievements of military engineering of the 20th century'. Motorbike it between the two cities (via Laos) for an epic Vietnamese end-to-end.

Essential information:
With over 61 million motorbikes on Vietnam's roads, you'll find repair shops, gas stations and food stops all along the way.

Far left to right: motorbike Vietnam on the Ho Chi Minh Trail; Cape Reinga, northern terminus of the Te Araroa trail; complete a continent-wide ride on the Tour d'Afrique

2

Te Araroa
New Zealand

Opened in 2011 after 35 years in the making, the 3000km (1860-mile) Te Araroa hiking trail links Cape Reinga, at the north of New Zealand's North Island, to Bluff at the south end of the South. This terrific tramp traverses forested and volcanic land – expect to scale mountains, cover river valleys, and trek through seven of the nation's cities via link sections alongside roads, as well as covering new walkways and ancient routes.

Essential information:
Allow 120 days to complete the full route.

3

Pan-American Highway
Multi-country

There's around 48,000km (29,800 miles) of road (and one small blip) between northern Alaska and Argentina's Tierra del Fuego. In short, this is the mother of all road trips; bar a Darién Gap detour in Panama, you can drive the entire length of the Americas. There is no one route. The original and only official section runs from Laredo in northern Mexico to Buenos Aires; multiple branches allow you to cover the full Arctic to (almost) Antarctic distance.

Essential information:
Crossing the Darién Gap region is not advisable due to the difficult terrain and safety risks.

4

Tour d'Afrique
Cairo to Cape Town

Spend four months cycling through 10 countries to traverse a whole continent. You could do it solo, but more fun is the annual Tour d'Afrique, an epic race for riders of all abilities. Some of what you'll see includes (ready?) Egypt's Karnak Temple; Tanzania's Ngorongoro Crater; the Great Rift Valley (known as the 'cradle of mankind'); waterfall supremo Victoria Falls; the wildlife-stuffed Okavango Delta; and Cape Town's crowning glory, Table Mountain.

Essential information:
Riders notch up 11,953km (7375 miles), hundreds of blisters and a lifetime of memories over a four-month period.

OAXACA IS HUMMING

Mya-Rose Craig finds a spiritual connection with birds in Mexico

I'm sitting on a whitewashed bench outside a rustic log cabin, looking out across the enormous tree-filled valley of the San José del Pacifico forest and contemplating what brought me to Oaxaca. More specifically, what brought me to this place. The town has long been notorious for one thing in particular: the hallucinogenic mushroom *Psilocybe mexicana*. While these wild shrooms have been ritually consumed for over 2000 years by the region's Indigenous population, stories of their potency began to attract visitors from the early 1960s onwards.

The draw for me, however, was rooted in an altogether different kind of trip. One where I hoped to find a spiritual connection with the Earth through my love of its birds. Like many people my age, life is busy with university, work and seeing friends. I'm an environmental campaigner, but I'm also a birdwatcher. Birding keeps me well. At the age of 13 I set up Black2Nature, inspired by my own experience as a young, non-white nature enthusiast, and opened up conversations on the things that prevent minority ethnic people from spending time in the countryside.

I love birds because they are so visible. Every landscape has them and, for me, birdwatching away from home is about immersing myself in the habitats that the birds require to survive, indulging in their beauty and gaining an understanding of the places they live in. In my memoir, *Birdgirl*, I wrote about the global birding trips I've been on. I want people to gain an understanding of why

I love these tiny creatures so much. And also that even though my passion for birds may border on obsession, anyone can enjoy birding. Many places in the Americas have hummingbird feeders at restaurants or in hotel gardens; the more adventurous of us can opt to explore on foot with a guide. Our guide in Oaxaca, Eric Antonio Martinez, is one of the best in the region, and he's the reason I've seen over 100 new birds here.

With over 1000 different bird species, and more than 120 that can only be seen within its borders, Mexico has long been a huge part of the world birdwatching scene, with US birders travelling south to seek exotic and rare species. Back in August 2016, I was watching hummingbirds at feeders during the Southeast Arizona Birding Festival when some fellow birders told me that since I loved this species, I should visit Mexico. They recommended bird guide Eric Antonio Martinez. I got in touch straight away with a list of all the hummingbirds that live in or pass through Mexico that I hadn't yet seen. A flurry of emails followed, where we discussed a potential itinerary. I threw myself into preparation mode. Where were the places to see these birds? What were their habitats? How could I identify them?

I started to feel anxious about doing a big volcano trek, so I began to train. We prepared lists, itineraries and maps. Into my bag went my binoculars and telescope, camera and carbon-fibre tripod. Then waterproofs, lightweight clothing, thermals, boots, waterproof socks, travel towel, silk liner and bars of soap.

We got settled in Oaxaca and left early in search of the secretive white-throated jay, which can only be observed in the vicinity of the humid forest that surrounded us. Eventually, we spotted two, but this was not to be the real highlight of my trip.

I had seen countless amazing hummingbirds during my last week here, from the amethyst-throated mountaingem to the white-bellied emerald, the Mexican violetear and the curve-winged sabrewing. But I was on my way back to my cabin when I saw the bird that was the true target of my trip. A miniature marvel, the bumblebee hummingbird is the third-smallest of its species in the world, at a miniscule 7cm (2.7in) long. This one buzzed past us and darted in amongst the vegetation. I managed to get a fantastic view of it hovering over a purple flower, gorging on its nectar. Metallic green on top, white underneath, with a glistening purple throat. I couldn't help but let out a gasp.

Like many natural spaces, Mexico is suffering under the damage from climate change and environmental degradation, and the birds are struggling, too. During my trip I saw many forms of deforestation. A site that Eric had been birding in only three months before, looking for the rare Sumichrast's wren, had disappeared entirely, chopped down to have its wood exported and replaced by crops.

I love watching birds around the world, but I genuinely believe that the money from tourism is the only practicable way to stop their extinction. And as a traveller, I choose to tread lightly.

COMPLETE A MARATHON

A challenge that takes months to train for, over in a few (mercifully) short hours. Any marathon changes you – because despite the agony, you know you're part of something huge. Humanity has swollen to more than the sum of its parts: the very best of people is on display, spectators and runners both. Make your marathon more interesting by taking on these five far-from-routine races for the ultimate travel challenge.

1

ANTARCTIC ICE MARATHON
Antarctica

The race: Subzero temperatures, katabatic winds, slippy terrain, altitude-thinned air – as if 26.2 miles wasn't testing enough! But running in such pristine wilderness, where the only sound is the crunch of your own (weary) feet, is a privilege indeed.

The stats
Coordinates: 79°47'S, 82°53'W (Union Glacier Camp)
When: December
Participants: 40
Profile: Largely flat, but run at altitude (700m/2297ft)
Temperature: -20°C/-4°F
Fee: US$19,500
Distance to the South Pole: 1000km (621 miles)
Average wind speed: 10-25 knots
Daylight: 24hrs
Probable calories burned: 10,000
Kit list: Thermal top, fleece, outer windproof shell, long johns, windproof trousers, gloves, mittens, two pairs of woollen socks, neoprene toe-covers, balaclava, facemask, hat, neck gaiter, goggles

2

BIG SUR MARATHON
California, USA

The race: The 26.2 miles from Big Sur Village to Carmel are prone to landslides, pea-soupers and ocean-brewed storms. But they also follow Hwy 1, one of the world's most dramatic roads. Hard work, yes, but drop-dead gorgeous too.

The stats
Coordinates: 36°6'N, 121°37'W (Big Sur)
When: April
Participants: 4500
Profile: Hilly, total ascent 300m (984ft); 13 hills in last 21km (13 miles)
Temperature: 10-15°C/50-59°F
Fee: Domestic US$265, international US$299
Porta-potties used: 385
Pre-race pasta party comprises: 113kg (250lb) of pasta, 189L (50 gallons) of marinara sauce
Proportion of waste material recycled or composted: Over 91%
Economic impact: US$18 million
Water supplied: 6340L (1675 gallons) at start and finish; 28,675L (7575 gallons) on course

3

THE GREAT WALL MARATHON
China

The race: Most of this route lies alongside China's beefy barricade, negotiating rice fields and remote villages in the Huangyaguan region. The section on the Wall itself is only 3.5km (2 miles) long but is completed twice and is malevolently memorable: 5164 punishingly steep steps. Note that the pandemic has caused the cancellation or changes to several events, such as this run.

The stats
Coordinates: 40°2'N, 117°23'E (Jixian)
When: September
Participants: 2000
Profile: Hilly, with 5164 steps
Temperature: 20-25°C/68-77°F
Fee: Starts at US$350
Gradient: Up to 10%
Oldest runner: 78
Bottles of water carried on foot to the Wall on race morning: 15,000
Year inaugurated: 1999

FROM 0–26.2 MILES...
... IN FOUR MONTHS

Marathons are won or lost in the months before the big day. If it's the week before your first marathon and you haven't trained, you may have bitten off more than you can chew. But for the modestly active person, four months of training will be enough to get you across the finish line.

Basic training schedule

Weeks 1 to 4
Three rest days per week, not consecutively
Two days per week: easy jog, increasing from 20min to 50min
One day per week: long run increasing from 40min to 70min
One day per week: gentle recovery run for 30min

Weeks 5 to 8
Three rest days per week, not consecutively
One day per week: steady run for 40min to 60min
One day per week: speed-running for 40min
One day per week: long run increasing from 80min to 16km (10 miles)
One day per week: gentle recovery run for 40min

Weeks 9 to 12
Three rest days per week, not consecutively
One day per week steady run for 40min to 60min

One day per week: speed-running for 50min
One day per week: long run increasing from 16km (10 miles) to 21km (13 miles) or a half-marathon race
One day per week: gentle recovery run for 40min

Weeks 13 to 15
Three rest days per week, not consecutively
One day per week: steady run for 40min to 60min
One day per week: speed-running for 50min
One day per week: long run decreasing from 32km (20 miles) to 13km (8 miles)
One day per week: gentle recovery run for 40min

Week 16
In the week before the race, taper your training and do only 2 x 30min easy runs and a 20min jog

---

4

JUNGFRAU MARATHON
Switzerland

The race: It doesn't actually go up the 3454m (11,332ft) Jungfrau, but this route from Interlaken (560m/1837ft) to Kleine Scheidegg (2060m/6758ft) is still a beautiful brute. It turns really vertiginous at 24km (the 15-mile mark), when 500m (1640ft) of ascent squeeze into a 5km (3-mile) zigzag. Breathtaking in every sense.

The stats
Coordinates: 46°41'N 7°51'E (Interlaken)
When: September
Participants: 4000
Profile: Extremely uphill – total ascent 1830m (6004ft); max altitude 2205m (7234ft)
Temperature: 10-20°C/50-68°F
Fee: CHF179 (US$180)
Elevation gain: 1823m (5981ft)
Course record: 2.49:01 (Jonathan Wyatt, New Zealand)
Time race distance takes by train: 1hr 15min (Interlaken–Kleine Scheidegg)
Best fuel: *Rösti* (fried grated potatoes), *birchermüesli*, Rivella (milk-whey soft drink)

5

LEWA MARATHON
Kenya

The race: Race the world's best long-distance runners AND the wildlife. This dust-track animal-infested 26.2-er crosses Lewa Conservancy, home to rhino, elephant, giraffe and buffalo. All good reasons to keep on moving...

The stats
Coordinates: 0°12'N, 37°25'E (Lewa Wildlife Conservancy)
When: June
Participants: 1000
Profile: Undulating, run at altitude (1700m/5577ft)
Temperature: 20-30°C/68-86°F
Fee: US$288 plus US$2020 charitable donation
Money raised for charity since inception: US$3.8 million
Animals potentially seen: Rhino, lion, leopard, buffalo, elephant, zebra, giraffe, oryx, ostrich and many more
Security: Armed rangers, Supercub light aircraft, surveillance helicopters
Chance of winning: 0% (past competitors include world-record-holding Kenyan elite runners)

"ALL I DO IS KEEP
MY OWN COZY,
MY OWN
SILENCE. AND
WONDERFUL
WHAT ANYBODY

ON RUNNING IN
HOMEMADE VOID,
NOSTALGIC
THIS IS A PRETTY
THING. NO MATTER
ELSE SAYS."

– HARUKI MURAKAMI, *WHAT I TALK
ABOUT WHEN I TALK ABOUT RUNNING*

VOLUNTEERING

'What is the essence of life? To serve others and to do good.' Greek philosopher Aristotle spoke these words over 2300 years ago and they still ring true. There is joy in service, and volunteering has long been a part of human culture. Travel – and the communities we visit – give us so much: adventure, healing, inspiration and life-altering experiences. Want to give in return? Travel with respect for planet and people, and lend a hand where you can.

1

Citzen science
Antarctica

Make a measurable impact – and your marine biologist dreams a reality – on a citizen science expedition, collecting data for the creation of the Antarctic Peninsula's first Marine Protected Area. Surrounded by raw nature at the ends of the Earth (yes, you'll see icebergs and, likely, penguins and whales), you'll accompany scientists studying marine life and the impacts of climate change. In the evenings, geek out at onboard expert lectures.

Essential information:
Given Antarctica's extreme conditions, opportunities are seasonal. Expeditions generally run between October and March.

2

Wildlife protection
Costa Rica

Costa Rica occupies just 0.03% of the planet's surface, but is home to nearly 6% of its biodiversity. From coast to coast, you can lend a hand with rescue, research, protection and rehabilitation. Work at a national park ranger station on the Osa Peninsula. Care for rescued sloths and monkeys at a Pacific Coast sanctuary. Help protect green macaws at Punta Islita breeding centre and Sarapiqui field station, or sea turtles in Parque Nacional Tortuguero.

Essential information:
The rainy season is lovingly called 'green season'. Even in drier months, some areas receive rain: come prepared with proper gear.

3

Women's empowerment
Bali

Contribute your time to NGOs providing training that empowers local women to qualify for higher-paid jobs, build businesses and improve the health of their families. You might help with language classes, health programmes, environmental education or business training; be open to learning, too, soaking up local knowledge, culture and traditions. In your downtime, hit the trails, relax in hot springs and immerse in cultural experiences.

Essential information:
Travellers can reach Bali via Ngurah Rai International Airport (also called Denpasar International Airport).

4

Environmental conservation
Australia

Get physical and contribute to conservation in spectacular settings. Dive into marine monitoring and clean-ups on the Great Barrier Reef. Reforest Queensland's Daintree Lowland Rainforest with native species alongside the Eastern Kuku Yalanji Bama Traditional Owners. Remove invasive species in New South Wales' Blue Mountains, or assist with bushfire recovery and bushcare in South Australia.

Essential information: Year-round opportunities are available. Australia's seasons are the opposite of the Northern Hemisphere: pack accordingly.

Clockwise, from top: squirrel monkey, Costa Rica; giving thanks in Bali; scouting the scene at Australia's Great Barrier Reef

Mary Anning —
the fossil woman

Some of the finest fossils in this gallery were found by Mary Anning (1799–1847) of Lyme Regis, Dorset. At the age of 11, she discovered a complete ichthyosaur skeleton in the Blue Lias rocks of Charmouth beach. Fossil hunting became a life-long passion, and Mary Anning earned respect from collectors and scientists alike. Sadly, the 'fossil woman' of Lyme Regis died of cancer at the age of 47.

Fossilised ichthyosaurs and plesiosaurs, preserved in Lower or Middle Jurassic rocks, have been found in many sites in southern England. Mary Anning is thought to be the first person to discover complete ichthyosaur and plesiosaur skeletons, and her remarkable fossils are still studied by scientists today.

Pliosaur
Rhomaleosaurus cromptoni

FIND
FOSSILS

Some 200 years ago, in the shale cliffs near Lyme Regis, on England's south coast, the teenage Mary Anning uncovered a 5m-long (16ft) skeleton of an ichthyosaur, a species that last walked the Earth 90 million years ago. She was the first person ever to find an entire skeleton (which is now in the British Museum).

There are many places around the world where fossils can be found, from Great White North fossil fields such as Burgess Shale in the Canadian Rockies to the Unesco Global Geopark in Zigong, China, or the beaches of Alum Creek State Park in Ohio, USA. And no, not all the good stuff has been unearthed yet. In 2022, fossil hunters scouring Compton Bay beach on the Isle of Wight, England, found the fossilised remains of a huge ancient croc – a spinosaur, measuring 10m (33ft) from top to tail – that found its way onto the beach after a cliff erosion.

GO
SOLO

'The act of leaving is the bravest and most beautiful of all,' wrote Swiss explorer and self-styled vagabond Isabelle Eberhardt. 'One is only free when alone.' More than 120 years later, these words still ring true: solo travel is one of life's greatest freedoms, all the more exhilarating because it is daunting. It prompts self-reliance and reflection, and challenges your preconceived ideas. For travellers today, there's a kaleidoscope of possibilities: being alone in a crowd in Tokyo, wild swimming in Slovenia or epic hikes in New Zealand.

1

Slovenia

Underexplored compared to its European neighbours, Slovenia's lighter crowds, hassle-free culture and small size promise easy and enriching solo travel. Capital Ljubljana has all the magic and stately architecture of Prague or Budapest – a picturesque castle, interweaving bridges, the rosy-pink buildings of Prešeren Square. Thanks to a reliable bus and train network, easy day trips abound, including to gorgeous Lake Bled and the charming town of Škofja Loka, or wild swimming at Lake Bohinj.

Essential information:
Pan-European flights reach Ljubljana's international airport; there are also trains from Budapest, Munich and Zürich.

Far left to right: wild-swimming perfection in Slovenia; neon dreams fulfilled in Tokyo; solo hiking in New Zealand's Fiordland National Park

2

Guatemala

Small in size but with mighty variety, Guatemala suits solo travellers seeking culture, contemplation or tropical wildlife. Reflect on the passage of time at Tikal's ancient temples (attractive Flores is an easy jumping-off point), experience traditional village life at stunning Atitlán crater lake, or day-trip to Pacaya volcano from Antigua. Crime stats scare off some, but most visit safely, supported by a small but inclusive community of backpackers.

Essential information:
Flights depart from US hubs including LA, New York and Chicago. A week allows a taste of Guatemala; stay longer for immersive travel.

3

New Zealand

Solo travellers raise no eyebrows in Aotearoa (the 'Land of the Long White Cloud'). It's easy to strike up conversation over a meat pie, but tourists are common enough that you can choose to blend in. Fiordland National Park beckons to solo road trippers and long-distance hikers (try the epic Milford Track); it's also easy to join group excursions and meet a temporary group of mates, whether bungy jumping at Taupo or taking a Lake Rotorua cruise.

Essential information:
Buses and trains link major cities; ferries connect the North and South islands. Reaching remote spots requires more planning.

4

Japan

There are many fantastic reasons to embrace being alone in Japan. Throw yourself into a bedazzling, disorienting *Lost in Translation* experience in Tokyo. Give rapt attention to a plate of grilled oysters on Miyajima Island, or sizzling *okonomiyaki* in Osaka. Experience the snow-muffled silence of Hokkaidō's ski fields, or visit the Hiroshima memorials in thoughtful quiet. By devoting your full attention, you'll have a brimming bank of long-lasting sensory memories.

Essential information:
The Japan Rail pass allows you to fly across the country by Shinkansen bullet train, and it's excellent value over a few days.

LISTEN TO THE SILENCE

We dare you to stop talking for a week. How about a month? Shhhh. We live in a loud world. From mornings of Zoom meetings to evenings scrolling TikTok, we spend most of our days talking or listening. What if we could just... stop? That's what silent retreats are all about. An increasingly popular type of getaway, they force us to make space for quiet. Though this can be uncomfortable at first, the benefits are many: reduced stress, better sleep and a greater understanding of who we really are – minus the noise.

1

Kripalu Center
Massachusetts, USA

In a former Jesuit seminary in the Berkshire mountains, this is one of America's oldest yoga centres, and its silent retreats include guided movement, journaling, healthy home-cooked meals and nature walks around the spacious grounds. Winter is a particularly delicious time here, with snow blanketing the hardwood forest and the pond frozen solid. You'll emerge calmer, more centred and, hopefully, better able to ignore the distractions of your phone.

Essential information:
Kripalu is a little over 2hr west of Boston and 3hr north of New York City by car, and offers three- or five-day silent retreats.

2

Shōganji Zen Retreat
Ojuki, Japan

Led by a Rinzai Zen monk, Shōganji gives visitors the chance to experience life in a 600-year-old Buddhist temple. In a rural village on the southern island of Kyushu, the retreat is surrounded by bamboo forest and ringed by rice paddies and citrus groves; the beach is close enough to hear the waves at night. You can be totally silent here, simply hiking, meditating and soaking in hot springs; or try non-silent pursuits like green-tea ceremonies and calligraphy.

Essential information:
Shōganji is near the city of Ōita, which has a domestic airport. The closest international airport is in Fukuoka, 3hr away by train.

3

Dhamma Sikhara
Dharamsala, India

Deep in the Dhauladhar Range of the Western Himalayas, this is one of India's many Vipassana retreats, all funded by donation only. The 10-day retreat here is no spa experience: Vipassana is a difficult, even gruelling practice of sitting in silence and stillness with discomfort until our minds learn to observe and accept without judgement. The gorgeous setting, in a high-altitude cedar forest, is one of few luxuries: expect dorm-like rooms and basic vegetarian food.

Essential information:
The centre is 2km (1.2 miles) outside McLeod Ganj, reachable by foot or auto-rickshaw. Dharamsala's airport has flights to Delhi.

4

Buddhist Retreat Centre KwaZulu-Natal, South Africa

At the head of a valley overlooking the Umkomaas River, the natural beauty of the location here is so stunning you'll hardly miss talking. Walk the meditation labyrinth, wander the mossy Zen gardens in the morning mist or go birdwatching and hiking in fragrant pine forests. You'll sleep in cottages or thatch-roof chalets and gather produce for delectable vegetarian food. The silent retreats are based on Buddhist principles, but are open to all.

Essential information:
The Centre, in Ixopo, can schedule shuttles from Durban, about 2hr away.

Clockwise, from top: embrace Zen silence at Japan's Shōganji or Massachusetts' Kripalu Center; the Umkomaas River near South Africa's Buddhist Retreat Centre

FOLLOW THE HERD

From around May, one million wildebeest trek across the Serengeti, Tanzania. It takes them more than a month to migrate, which means that you can join them on their journey at various intervals along the route.

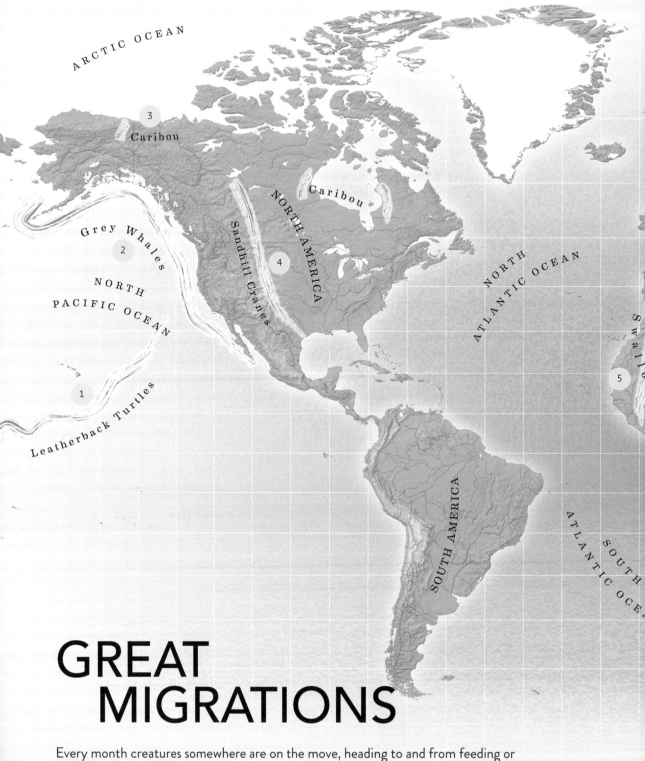

ARCTIC OCEAN

3
Caribou

Caribou

NORTH AMERICA

2
Grey Whales

NORTH
PACIFIC OCEAN

Sandhill Cranes

4

1
Leatherback Turtles

NORTH
ATLANTIC OCEAN

Swallo

5

SOUTH AMERICA

SOUTH
ATLANTIC OCEI

GREAT MIGRATIONS

Every month creatures somewhere are on the move, heading to and from feeding or
birthing grounds, or a rendezous with more of their kind. These are some of the most
extraordinary wildlife spectacles in the world. Here are 10 of the best to witness.

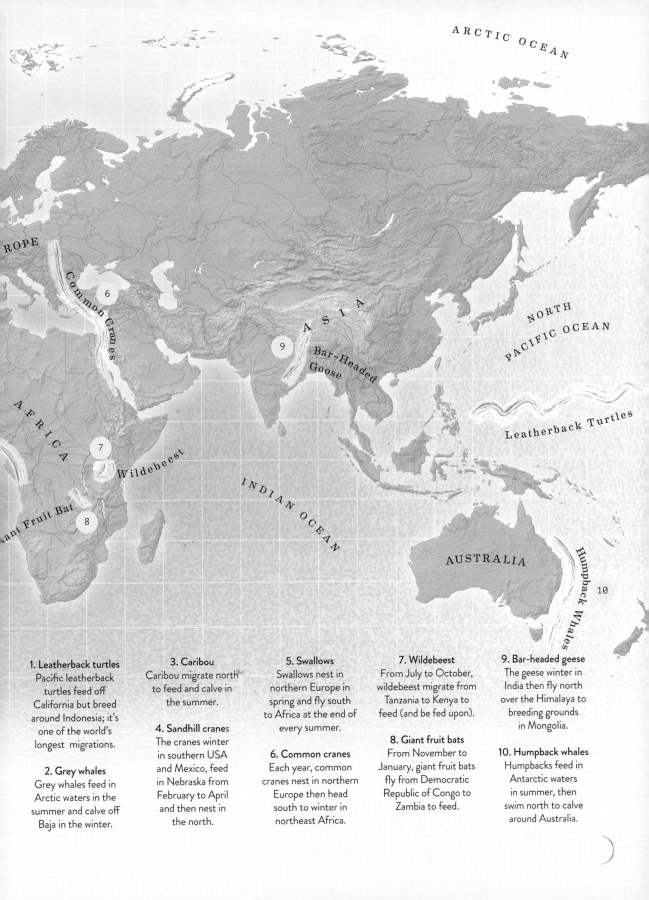

ARCTIC OCEAN

EUROPE

ASIA

NORTH
PACIFIC OCEAN

Common Cranes

6

9

Bar-Headed
Goose

AFRICA

7

Leatherback Turtles

Wildebeest

Giant Fruit Bat

8

INDIAN OCEAN

AUSTRALIA

Humpback Whales

10

1. Leatherback turtles
Pacific leatherback turtles feed off California but breed around Indonesia; it's one of the world's longest migrations.

2. Grey whales
Grey whales feed in Arctic waters in the summer and calve off Baja in the winter.

3. Caribou
Caribou migrate north to feed and calve in the summer.

4. Sandhill cranes
The cranes winter in southern USA and Mexico, feed in Nebraska from February to April and then nest in the north.

5. Swallows
Swallows nest in northern Europe in spring and fly south to Africa at the end of every summer.

6. Common cranes
Each year, common cranes nest in northern Europe then head south to winter in northeast Africa.

7. Wildebeest
From July to October, wildebeest migrate from Tanzania to Kenya to feed (and be fed upon).

8. Giant fruit bats
From November to January, giant fruit bats fly from Democratic Republic of Congo to Zambia to feed.

9. Bar-headed geese
The geese winter in India then fly north over the Himalaya to breeding grounds in Mongolia.

10. Humpback whales
Humpbacks feed in Antarctic waters in summer, then swim north to calve around Australia.

CATCH A WAVE

Live the dream: learn to catch waves, day after endless day. Sure, you showed up at the beach without a clue about board wax, goofy stance or riptides. But after a few days of surf lessons, you were catching waves. That first day, your instructor pushed you hard. Then, they didn't have to tell you what to do. The waves seemed limited and the time was now. Your instincts kicked in and your brain turned off. You felt the swells and communed with the vastness of the ocean.

1

Glitz & glam
Biarritz, France

Sure, holidaying French royals have made Biarritz a famously posh destination for centuries. But it's the surfers who dominate the scene today, especially during July's surf competition. You seamlessly slip into the stream by taking surf and French lessons rolled into one, forgetting the pain of the subjunctive as you glide toward shore in perfect balance. North of Pointe St-Martin, Anglet's adrenaline-pumping surf beaches continue for miles. Toast your achievements with a glass of champagne.

Essential information: Take bus 10 from the bottom of av Verdun (near av Édouard VII).

Far left to right: ready for the breaks in Biarritz, France; the gorgeous beaches of Biarritz have long been a favourite of royals; surfing Costa Rica

2

Into the wild
Noosa Beach, Australia

North of Brisbane on the Sunshine Coast, Noosa Beach reigns as one of Australia's premier surf spots, and Merrick's is one of the most popular surf schools. As part of the Noosa National Park, the beaches here feel wild. You may even spot a native koala hanging about in the trees as you carry your board to the break. And you'll certainly never forget learning to catch smooth, glossy waves in the ridiculously turquoise waters here.

Essential information:
Merrick's offers super-fun 2hr group lessons twice daily, as well as the option of private tutorials.

3

Tropical paradise
Playa Guiones, Costa Rica

You're the kind of newbie surfer who wants to take lessons within sight of palm fronds – in the tropics. But you like the quiet side of the tropics, a place with surf schools, but where the jungle creeps through every crack. That's why you learn to ride the waves of the crescent-shaped Playa Guiones in Nosara, Costa Rica. There you commune with likeminded surfers from around the world, who totally get your vibe.

Essential information:
The beach break is best when there's an offshore wind. Guiones is usually busy, but has ample take-off points.

4

Big appetites
San Sebastián, Spain

When you catch a wave in San Sebastián, you can also catch a glimpse of its handsome low skyline. This Basque city is a serious surf destination, but one that focuses equally on food and nightlife. Enjoy the predictable waves and a soft sandy beach during the day, and then indulge at San Sebastián's best *pintxo* restaurants after the sun sets. Surfers head one beach over to the powerful waves that roll in towards Playa de la Zurriola.

Essential information:
The waves in summer are smaller and more suited to beginners; winter works for intermediate surfers.

LESSONS IN LIVING LIGHTLY

Sarah Barrell goes back to basics

We break camp early; the sun has yet to burn the mist off the treetops. Our campfire is still smouldering despite the insistent humidity that's already made wet rags of my shirt. Segundo, my Indigenous Huitoto guide, deftly helps me unhook my hammock and mosquito net from the trees, scuffs out the fire, and we step wordlessly out onto a jungle path towards the river. I glance back through the trees to where we'd spent the night, rain tip-tapping on our hammock awnings, and Segundo's voice conjuring Huitoto legends of snakes, floods and vengeful gods. Our home for the night in the Colombian Amazon, larger than life under the blanket of darkness, is now untraceable.

Segundo strides out under the dripping forest canopy. I trot sweatily behind. Besides the hammocks he carries nothing. Around his waist, a hip pouch contains not much more than his *mambe* (coca powder) and tobacco. My knapsack of essentials comprises a sarong, a couple of T-shirts, token mozzie spray (the bites continue regardless), some toiletries (rarely used unless near a river), a sleeping bag, water and a camera. Most of my belongings had been dumped in a lock-up in Leticia, the closest Amazon hub town. Mobile phone? There's no reception. Rain mac? What's the point, perspiration will drench you first. Wallet? Banks and shops are far away.

The very first time I trekked and camped in the Amazon, some 15 years previously, it felt like heading for incarceration. Bound for the densely forested banks of Peru's Tambopata, seven hours upriver from the nearest town, I had handed over keys, phone and wallet to a lockup and, with them, a significant sense of self. But what I found, in fact, was that this led to liberation rather than confinement. Without these fidgety fixtures of modern identity, I was free to just be.

Then, as now, my hosts equipped me with all I needed. I am directed to trees that produce water, to twigs that double as toothbrushes, to a directory of flora with medical attributes. Within a 3-sq-metre (32-sq-ft) tract of forest, with the right knowledge, you could treat everything from cuts and abrasions to diarrhoea, arthritis and impotence. What you need here is not technical kit and clothing but know-how. Segundo navigates swiftly through seemingly impenetrable walls of rainforest like a man with an inner GPS, delivering us, suddenly, to a *chacra* – one of the Amazon's small subsistence farms. It's as if he has just produced a rabbit from a huge, shrub-filled hat.

The forest is very much alive, a physical and spiritual entity governed by gods who must be appeased. Become cavalier at your peril; the trees here may take their revenge. Strangler figs and mangroves form gothic cages around you, 'walking' palms block your path, and vines seethe around your ankles, sprouting back minutes after your machete's slash. Everyone, it seems, has a hair-raising tale of a friend missing all night on a route they walked daily.

But this morning, all are present and correct in the *maloca*, the traditional palm-thatch longhouse at the centre of this *chacra*. Abuelo, the community's elder, is going about morning chores, frying eggs and corn for breakfast, shadowed by the resident pack of skinny pups. Tending to crops here must be like pruning a bramble patch with nail clippers, and yet the *chacra* ia abundant with corn, yam, pineapple and banana. Natural pest control comes by way of the weaver birds and caciques that prey on insects, nesting in one or two strategically planted trees.

Here is a wild world made manageable – not tamed, but tacitly understood. And filled with age-old processes that are simple yet skilled and completely sustainable – a metaphor for a life lived lightly.

" WHAT IS PERTINENT
OF THAT BEAUTY,
RESTRAINT. IT IS
LAND KNOWS OF ITS
ITS OWN GREATNESS,
NEED TO

IS THE CALMNESS
ITS SENSE OF
AS THOUGH THE
OWN BEAUTY, OF
AND FEELS NO
SHOUT IT."

– KAZUO ISHIGURO, *THE REMAINS OF THE DAY*

COMMIT TO COMMUNITY

You can become part of a community without living there full-time, by making friends on a visit and then supporting it remotely. Respecting local communities is a crucial part of travel. With everyone pulling together, like these dragon boat racers on Lake Liyu in Taiwan, we'll get where we need to go.

CHAPTER 5

A YEAR

KNOW
YOUR PLACE

Contemplate your place in the universe while stargazing somewhere like Lake Taupo, New Zealand. The images being received from the James Webb telescope put our own lives in perspective among the mind-scrambling scale of the cosmos but also highlight how important it is to preserve our own precious planet.

WORK
YOUR WAY

Why work at home when you could work on a yacht? Perhaps you want to spend a year backpacking, but you lack the funds. Or maybe you're just hankering for a change of scenery. Either way, a job-hopping travel year might be the ticket. Pick apples in the Southern Hemisphere before cruising north to tend a hostel bar in Germany; or teach scuba in Thailand for the winter then spend the summer crewing a yacht through the Greek isles. Beats sitting behind a screen, right?

1

Crew a yacht

Running a yacht takes a lot of people. You need captains and first mates, of course, but also cooks and stewards and deckhands and cleaners. That's where you come in. Crew are often hired seasonally or by journey, making it a perfect gig for the travelling-while-working lifestyle. Island-hop through French Polynesia, then disembark and fly to France for a transatlantic crossing on a different vessel. While not all jobs require experience, you will need a short basic training course and medical certification.

Essential information: Yacht owners seek crew on websites like crewfinders.com. Registering with a yacht club is another good route.

2

Pick fruit

Agricultural labour might not sound like much fun, but the right gig can deliver not just cash, but a sense of community. Apple-picking in New Zealand is a popular choice for backpackers looking to settle for a few months. The work is hard, but evenings mean group-cooked meals at the guesthouse and stories from all over the world. Or join the autumn grape harvest in France, taking part in an ancient tradition, complete with free accommodation (and some free wine!).

Essential information: Many countries allow international fruit pickers to work as part of a working holiday visa.

3

Be an au pair

Like kids? Families around the world seek au pairs; young travellers who become a temporary part of the family while caring for the children. The gigs mean room and board, pocket money, and – often – travel with the family on their holidays. Many European countries limit working hours to 30 per week, which means you'll have plenty of time for sightseeing and lounging in cafes. Plus, if you're looking to learn another language, kids make some of the best practice partners.

Essential information: Au pair requirements vary by country, but often have upper age limits of 30. An agency can connect you with jobs.

4

Teach skiing

Got ski skills? Become an instructor, spending winters in the Alps, the Rockies or northern Japan. Days on the slopes watching kids (or adults) fall on their snow-suited butts turn into nights of hot toddies in the chalet with coworkers from across the globe. Days off mean fresh powder for hours. Seasons can last from a few months to nearly half a year, depending on location. If you're really keen, trade northern hemisphere winter for southern – both Argentina and Chile have excellent skiing.

Essential information: Many resorts have in-house training, while others require certifications.

Far left to right: crewing a yacht can be a perfect work-travel gig; fund ongoing travels with a season of fruit picking; live amid powdery slopes via a spell as a ski instructor

SAY YES

David Cornthwaite is the 'yes' man.

After an incredible 156 days and a sole-searing 5823km (3618 miles), I finally rolled into Brisbane, smashing two world records in the process. I'd traversed the whole of Australia, from Perth on the west coast, across the never-ending Nullarbor Plain, to the eastern shore. On... a skateboard.

Following my graduation from university, I had found a job fast, accepted it without thinking and lapsed into a disenchanted life of ennui and materialism. After 18 months I awoke with a feeling of moderate anger, something that drove me to buy a long skateboard – with the original intention of improving my snowboarding skills.

After two weeks of skating around town, I started to see my familiar world from a different perspective and I developed an urge to explore. I skated to work, put the keys on the desk, quit my job and promised myself that I'd skate further than anyone else ever had. One year later I became the first person to skate the length of Britain. Within two

years, I was setting off for Australia. Shortly after I arrived in Brisbane, my phone rang – and I was asked to write a book. I said yes. And from there, I set about saying yes, a lot.

I created Expedition1000, a project of 25 journeys of 1600km (1000 miles) or more, each using a different form of non-motorised transport. I said yes to paddling from source to sea down the Murray River; riding a tandem bike 2253km (1400 miles) between Vancouver and Vegas; paddleboarding over 3862km (2400 miles) along the Mississippi; swimming down the Missouri River; sailing across the Pacific on a 22m (72ft) yacht; and riding an elliptical bicycle 3219km (2000 miles) across Europe.

But adventure doesn't necessarily mean painfully long and difficult journeys. Saying yes doesn't mean you have to quit your job or sell your house or buy a tent. It's just a very effective means of slowing time, by weighing it down with experiences we really want to have – rather than those we feel we should.

WORK ON
THE GO

Because the 'home' in 'work from home' can be anywhere, right? More than ever, jobs are untethered from physical location. So why make a butt-shaped dent in your couch when you could be working from a hammock in Fiji? You can see the world without draining your bank account, and get a deeper feel for your location than if you visited on holiday. You don't need to limit yourself to one place, though. Spend six months in one country, then hop to another, with nothing but your laptop and your sense of adventure.

1

Croatia

Combining sunny Med vibes with Old World architecture, Croatia is a top spot for digital nomads: the country is enticing remote workers with a 12-month visa programme. Just show proof of income, fill out a few forms, and the next thing you know you'll be sipping *rakija* (Croatian brandy) in a cafe overlooking a pebbly beach, or working on a laptop in a coffee bar in fun, funky Zagreb. You'll find plenty of other international nomads to hike, swim and explore with during your off hours.

Essential information:
Zagreb has the country's biggest airport, followed by those at Dubrovnik, Split and Zadar.

Far left to right: become part of the cafe culture in Zagreb, Croatia; take time off at Curaçao's Cas Abao Beach; living the digital nomad life

2

Curaçao

Type away in your fragrant garden as hummingbirds flit around you, the soft sound of Caribbean waves providing white noise. This Dutch-affiliated island has opened itself up to remote workers via its '@HOME in Curaçao' programme, aimed at US and Dutch passport-holders but available to other nationalities too. After work, explore the crayon-coloured capital, Willemstad; hike windy bluffs amid cacti and watapana trees; or snorkel neon-turquoise waters at Cas Abao Beach.

Essential information:
Curaçao International Airport has direct flights to Amsterdam and many North and South American cities.

3

Thailand

Thailand has long been the digital nomad's country of choice. Natural splendour, spectacular food and a relatively low cost of living make it an excellent spot to set up shop for the medium- to long-haul. The country is actively courting remote workers – a new 10-year 'work from Thailand' visa is aimed at drawing skilled workers to the country. Rent an apartment in Phuket and spend your workday with your feet in the sand – sure beats that sad couch back home, doesn't it?

Essential information:
Thailand has no shortage of airports, so you'll be able to pop away for the weekend to almost any international destination.

4

Brazil

South America's first country to offer a digital nomad visa, Brazil lets international workers stay for up to a year. And oh, what a year you'll have. Here you can sip caipirinhas on Ipanema Beach, learn to surf in the bayside town of Praia do Rosa, scream for your team at Rio's Maracanã football stadium, track jaguars in the Pantanal wetlands... oh, yeah, and maybe do a little work too. Whether you base yourself in a big city or a beachside hamlet, you'll enjoy a healthy helping of the *vida boa* (good life).

Essential information:
Brazil is South America's biggest country, so do some research about which city or province might suit you.

A COMMEMORATIVE JOURNEY

Maggie Downs lets the good times roll in memory of her mother

It's just after 11pm when the bartender tips my bottled beer into a plastic cup and shoves me out the door. I'm startled, and so are my new friends – a motley crew of other backpackers I met a few days ago on a bus through the Laos countryside.

This is how we learn that businesses in Luang Prabang must close by 11.30pm every night. Doors are locked, windows are shuttered. Curfew begins at midnight, turning this picturesque place into more of a ghost town.

Along the mile-long (1.6km) walk to our hostel, we hear whispers. The streets are nearly empty, but there are men on the corners, skulking in the shadows.

'Psst!'

They ask if we want to go bowling. Their voices are husky, secretive. My friends and I agree: 'bowling' is obviously code, but for what? Opium den? Sex show? Something wild we can't even imagine? We decline and stroll away, puzzled, into the inky night.

My new backpacker buddies are on holiday, but I'm nine months into a solo trip around the world. I was inspired to do this by my mum, who longed for adventure but never booked the trip. She put things off, assuming there'd be time later. Then she was diagnosed with Alzheimer's disease before she could get one passport stamp closer to her dreams.

When my mum reached the final stages of her illness, I quit my newspaper job, sold my stuff and began travelling, making the trip she couldn't. The journey has already taken me along the Inca Trail to Machu Picchu, on safari in South Africa, rafting the Nile River in Uganda and volunteering with elephants in Thailand. Now, here.

Other than the strangers' whispered offers, Luang Prabang after dark is calm and serene, ruffled only by chirping insects and the shimmy of a breeze. The city glows with lanterns, illuminating dollhouse villas, gold-edged temples and gentle hills. My mum would have loved it.

A few days pass and my friends and I are out again. After a rousing evening of watery beer and board games, we're having so much fun that we want the night to become elastic, to stretch even just a couple hours longer, to go as far as it can possibly go. The closer the curfew creeps, the more determined we are to maintain this feeling. We can't possibly return to the quiet hostel. Not yet.

When a man calls out, 'Psst, bowling?' I pause.

Would my mum want me to take up a stranger's offer? No. But would my mum want me to say yes to adventure? Yes to life?

'Yes', I tell the man. YES TO BOWLING.

He exhales a long, low whistle to someone in a nearby cab. The vehicle is battered and smells dank and sweaty. My friends and I clamber inside.

The cab speeds outside the city limits, and I realise I have no idea where this steamy summer night in Laos will take us. I'm not afraid, though. I've been travelling long enough to know I can't escape the constant thrum of fear: being vulnerable is the nature of being human. I also know that staying home didn't protect my mum. Sometimes you simply have to see where the road leads.

Twenty minutes later, the cab screeches to a halt in front of a dark, warehouse-like building. We pay the man, and he drives away. Our only option is to go inside. One friend strides forward with a confident walk. He yanks the door open.

Inside the warehouse is the one thing I didn't expect – a bowling alley. Twelve gleaming lanes, glossy balls, the whole bit.

The place resembles every bowling alley I've ever seen in my life. There's the satisfying smack of the ball making contact with wood, the clatter of pins, the smell of smoke mingled with acrid socks. It's also packed with laughing, joyful bowlers.

This, it turns out, is the epicentre of nightlife in Luang Prabang. While the curfew keeps people off the streets past midnight, it doesn't stop them from letting the good times roll. Though the front wall is lined with the familiar adorably ugly red, green and white

bowling shoes, everyone has kicked their sandals off, and they've taken over the lanes with bare feet. We join them.

Pop music blares from tinny speakers, and many Laotians sing along. I do my best to chime in, and some guys in the next lane over poke fun at me. I smile and warble louder. It's all good fun: warm whiskey, bouncy music, terrible scores and gutter balls. We don't leave the bowling alley until morning. Remarkably, our cab has returned and is waiting for us.

The city is dense with mist, slinking through the trees and draping the hills like lace. The monks are sleepy-eyed, heading to the road in saffron robes to begin the daily alms walk. My body thrills to be in this moment, this dazzling place, and in the infinite possibility that comes from saying 'yes'.

"AT ANY GIVEN MOMENT
THERE'S A MILLION
IN THE BLURRING OF THE

IN THE MIDDLE OF A CITY
EPIPHANIES OCCURRING,
WORLD BEYOND THE CURTAIN"

– KAE TEMPEST, 'LIONMOUTH DOOR
KNOCKER', *LET THEM EAT CHAOS*

LEARN A NEW LANGUAGE

Aprende un idioma. Apprendre une langue. कोई भाषा सीखो. 學習一門語言. You might have heard that you can never learn a new language perfectly after childhood. Well, forget perfect. Learning a new language – messily, with a bad accent – is one of life's great growth experiences, and the lack of perfection is simply part of the joy. Apps and textbooks can only get you so far: to truly dig in, you've got to go for full immersion. Luckily the world is full of language schools ready to help learners at all levels.

1

Uttarakhand
India

In the foothills of the Himalaya, Landour Language School has been teaching Hindi and other Indian languages to non-natives for nearly 120 years. Sip a steaming cup of chai in the cool morning before settling down for lessons in an old stone church. Courses are either full- or half-day, the latter leaving your afternoons free for hiking through cedar forests filled with birdsong, or visiting temples, gardens and other local sites. Programmes are available for beginners through to advanced.

Essential information: Landour is in a suburb of Mussoorie. The nearest airport is in Dehradun, a short bus ride away.

2

Oaxaca
Mexico

The southwestern Mexican state of Oaxaca is justifiably famous for its language schools. People flock here to learn Spanish by day while exploring Oaxaca City by night. The cuisine is a major draw – nibble crunchy, savoury *tacos de chapulines* (cricket tacos), sip cinnamon-and-chilli-spiked hot chocolate, and tuck into chicken smothered in rich *mole* sauce. And then, of course, there's the mezcal, the local cactus-based liquor – one shot will make your Spanish 50% better (you'll think so, anyway)!

Essential information: There are dozens of language schools in Oaxaca, many of which can connect you with homestays.

3

Vermont
USA

Wait, what? Vermont? Yes, indeed, the tiny New England state best known for maple syrup is home to Middlebury College, which hosts one of the world's preeminent summer language schools. Whether you're a beginner or near-fluent, you can practise any of a dozen languages here, from Chinese, Hebrew, Portuguese and Arabic to Abenaki (spoken by Indigenous peoples of the northeastern US and Quebec). You'll be expected to speak in your target language at all times.

Essential information: Middlebury programmes run from two to eight weeks, and mean living in dorms, with group meals and activities.

4

Paris
France

Some classic experiences just shouldn't be messed with: spending spring in Paris learning French is one of them. In the cobblestone-paved Quartier Latin, the Alliance Française Paris is one of the best-known options: courses vary from evening intros to full-time intensives, plus a full slate of extracurricular social fun. Supplement your learning with browsing the *marchés aux puces* (flea markets) and French arthouse films at Le Champo.

Essential information:
The Alliance Française Paris runs courses year-round, but there are dozens, if not hundreds, of other schools.

Clockwise, from top: book a French course in Paris, with downtime exploring the markets and the city; Oaxaca's cuisine is as much of a draw as its language schools

TRAVEL ON TWO WHEELS

Silent, sustainable and as swift or slow as you feel like travelling, the bicycle is an increasingly popular way of exploring the world. Long-distance routes, often on quieter roads and tracks, criss-cross countries and continents, and with a bit of planning it's possible break them into perfectly-sized sections for the time you have, by connecting public transport hubs. Cycle-touring – or bikepacking as it's also known – connects travellers more closely with local communities and supports their economies.

1

La Vélodyssée
France

Hugging almost the entire west coast of France, this signposted cycle route is a classic voyage stretching from Roscoff in Brittany to Hendaye on the border with Spain. In the north the riding features short, sharp climbs around the coast's inlets and estuaries. Southward, glide from one surf beach to the next on sandy bike paths. Stopping and savouring the food and drink is part of the experience.

Essential information:
The distance is 1250km (776 miles) and there are good public transport hubs to break up the trip.

Far left to right: pedalling beside beaches on a Vélodyssée; Cape Reinga, starting point of the Tour Aotearoa; decorative dragons on a temple in Taipei, Taiwan

2

East Coast Greenway
USA

This work-in-progress will extend along the eastern seaboard of the US, from Florida to Maine. Around one third is complete and presently the best of the riding is through Maine, from Kittery to Calais, covering 590km (367 miles). The Greenway connects bike paths, rail trails and quiet roads to link urban and rural communities so you'll pass through natural scenery and cities such as Portland.

Essential information:
The entire route will be about 4828km (3000 miles) but for now focus on Maine.

3

Cycle Route 1
Taiwan

Circling the whole of Taiwan, this route is an unforgettable way of exploring this friendly island. It's pitched as an easy-going route, avoiding the mountainous interior, but don't underestimate the heat and humidity nor the challenges of navigating in a different language. The rewards for pedalling the mostly traffic-free bike paths are ocean views, hot springs and countless temples.

Essential information:
the route covers 965km (600 miles) but good public transport means you can do specific sections at a time.

4

Tour Aotearoa
New Zealand

If your quest is to cycle the entire length of a country, then this route through both the North and South Islands of New Zealand is the one to do first. It's an epic trip, taking in the golden beaches and giant trees of the north and the alpine scenery of the south. Designed by the Kennett brothers to connect as many of New Zealand's purpose-built bike trails, it's reasonably easy to complete sections at a time.

Essential information:
The full ride is around 3200km (1990 miles) but you can chose between two alternative routes down the South island.

KNOW YOURSELF

There's no more important journey to take than the one that helps you to get to know yourself. What are your hopes and your fears? How can you manage both? Do you prefer perpetual motion like this nomadic life in Kyrgyzstan, or to set down roots in one place?

ALL AROUND THE WORLD

The Austronesians of Southeast Asia and the Pacific were the first maritime sailors who travelled west to east, island-hopping by boat to cross the Pacific between China and the Americas thousands of years ago. From then onwards, circumnavigations have inspired people to set out from their front door to see the world: discover how some have succeeded (or not) by boat, plane or bicycle.

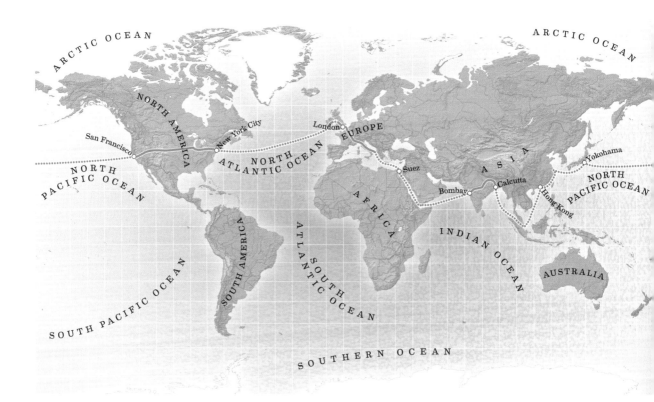

AROUND THE WORLD IN 80 DAYS
PHILEAS FOGG

Not all laps of the world actually happened. The popularity of Jules Verne's story, featuring globetrotter Phileas Fogg and his French valet Passepartout, is partly down to the rollicking good quality of the tale, but it's also attributable to brilliant timing. The novel was published in 1873, just after transcontinental railways had been completed in India and America, and the Suez Canal had opened: suddenly the world had become a much smaller place. This captured Verne's imagination, and the French author's portrayal of an Englishman betting £20,000 (£1.5 million in modern terms) that he could circle the globe in 80 days was a winner with armchair adventurers. In the tale, Fogg and Passepartout travel mostly via train and boat. Fogg never existed, of course, but in 1889 an intrepid American journalist called Nellie Bly did a circumnavigation of the planet in 72 days (seven days faster than Michael Palin managed 100 years later) using the same methods of transport.

BY BICYCLE
ALASTAIR HUMPHREYS' TWO-WHEELED TRIP

Before he got into micro-adventures, British explorer Alastair Humphreys took on some major macro-missions, the first of which was a mammoth circumnavigation of the planet by bicycle. Starting from his back door in Yorkshire in 2001, he pedalled 74,000km (45,981 miles) through 60 countries, traversing five continents to arrive back home in time for tea, just over four years later. His route was designed to take in countries that interested him, rather than to set any sort of speed record, as the map shows. He left his watch behind, rose with the sun and frequently collapsed into slumber in a wild-camping spot at dusk. Humphreys made a point of having conversations with local people wherever he went, and along the way ate a sheep's head, guinea pig, bear, sea urchin, horse, fried worms and scorpions. He rode with a granny-style basket on the front of his bike, discovered that car drivers are far more dangerous than both lions and bandits, and picked up enough language skills to convince Japanese police not to arrest him for cycling naked. Mission successful.

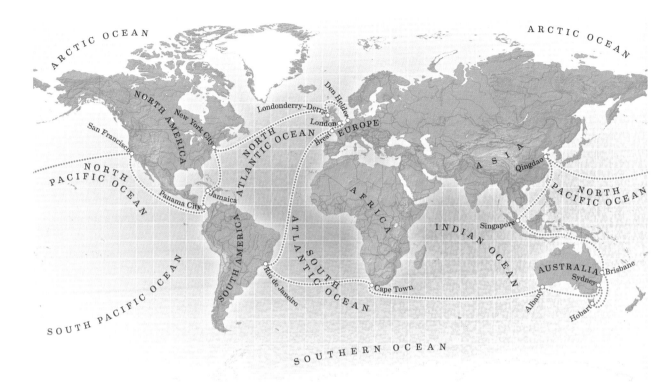

BY BOAT
CLIPPER ROUND-THE-WORLD RACE

In the Clipper Race, teams of amateur sailors go head-to-head in an epic 64,000km (39,768-mile) contest. Sailing identical yachts, the fleet departs from London's St Katharine Docks and follows a set route back to Britain. The Clipper was dreamt up in 1995 by Sir Robin Knox-Johnston, winner of the Jules Verne Trophy for being the first person to single-handedly sail around the planet without stopping. The 2018 race saw Wendy Tuck become the first female skipper to win it; in the same year, 25-year-old Nikki Henderson became the youngest skipper to take part. And previous races have seen drama aplenty: during the 2013–14 challenge, 12 boats duked it out on a course that sent them to France, Brazil, South Africa, Australia, Singapore, China, the US, Panama, Jamaica, Northern Ireland and the Netherlands. One sailor had a brush with death, falling overboard in heavy weather and floundering in the Pacific for 90 minutes. The threat of piracy plagued them on some stretches, while icebergs menaced in others, but all made it home.

BY PLANE
AMELIA EARHEART'S LAST FLIGHT

Some circumnavigations don't succeed. On 2 July 1937, Amelia Earhart was two-thirds of the way around the planet on a pioneering small-plane flight. As Earhart rolled her twin-engine Lockheed Electra down a jungle runway in Lae, New Guinea, the Americas were in her rear-view mirror, along with Africa, the Middle East and Australia. Next to her sat Fred Noonan, a specialist in celestial navigation, but the weather was dire and ahead lay 11,265km (7000 miles) of Pacific Ocean, punctuated only by slivers of terra firma. A smudge of land called Howland Island was their target. Three ships nearby were burning their lights to aid with navigation. One of these, the *Itasca*, had been receiving messages from Earhart for hours, but couldn't reply. At 7.42am they heard Earhart say: 'We must be on you, but we cannot see you. Fuel is running low.' An hour later, one more message: 'We are running north and south.' Then silence. The aviatrix disappeared without trace.

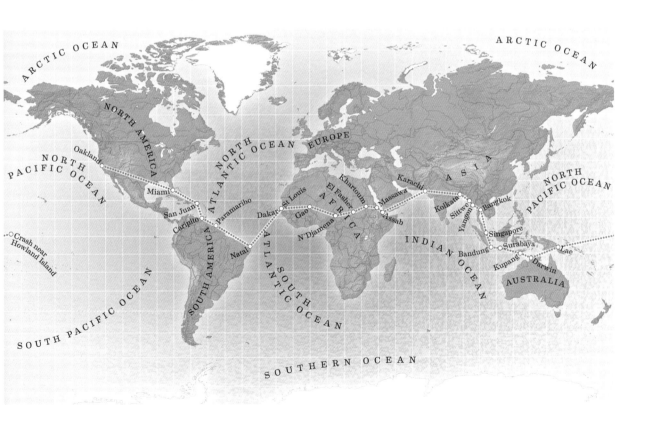

LEARN TO FREEDIVE

If skydiving is about the adrenalin rush of freefall, then freediving is the opposite: it's about finding and focusing on an inner kernel of serenity that comes through controlling your breathing and your emotions, without all the equipment of scuba diving weighing you down. Freediving is one of the world's fastest-growing sports, in part because of the feeling of empowerment that comes from defying human physiology. For many people, it's is a lifelong obsession: Mandy-Rae Cruickshank holds 13 Canadian freediving records and seven world records, including reaching 136m (446ft) in a no-limits freedive, holding a static apnea time of 6 minutes and 25 seconds, and freediving to 50m (164ft) without fins. Phew! But perhaps start with fins and snorkel while you test the water.

TAKING HOME
WITH YOU

Faren Rajkumar lives out life on the road in the USA.

The vanlife movement is celebrated as a fresh, new way to live, travel and even work wherever you choose. I agree that the choice certainly feels new every day: living and travelling in a van for several years with my partner – witnessing every season change in different corners of the US – is a huge departure from my previously predictable life as a graduate student. But what I've learned from life on the road is that the modern nomad is nothing new; I am a singular, breathing embodiment of humanity's attempt to get back to its earthy origins. There is a reason vanlife communities and families are growing in size, and in media recognition: we are tapping into collective, ancient nomadic roots and remembering what it means to wander the Earth together.

My van-dwelling partner and I are self-proclaimed hippies, and we'll gladly accept all the connotations. We're two brown-skinned people in colourful clothes doing yoga on the van roof, still young enough to feel like we'll live forever in our little red van in the forest. Home is our 2000 Ford Econoline called Shanti – true to her name, our van brings us peace. Even when we are too dusty, tired or cold, she is reliably present to either carry us to the next destination or cradle us to sleep for the night.

My transition from a traditional life in the suburbs of Florida was abrupt – it took me just a few weeks to decide to leave graduate school and move into a van after my first real road trip on the West Coast. Between the climbing and the ocean breeze and the countless friendly van-dwellers living on the Pacific Coast Highway, I was hooked. I quickly realised I had always been comfortable with less, and downsizing my life in terms of possessions and plans freed up my headspace for more magical ideas and daring.

Our little red van has seen us through five years of unexpected situations and redefined the meaning of travel. During the pandemic, I resisted my nomadic nature when fear took hold, and we quarantined in an apartment for two months, waiting for the world to end. When it didn't end, our feet were the first to revolt. They got itchy, and we had to hit the road before we went mad. The three months of meandering that followed took us through Wyoming, Montana, Idaho, Oregon, Colorado and Utah. My world exploded with possibility as I found myself brewing tea by a campfire under the stars, sitting humbly at the base of mountain peaks above 4260m (14,000ft) in the Tetons.

The joy brought up memories that originally motivated me to choose this life. I remembered that on my first van road-trip, I woke up in a van buried by pure, powdery snow to see the massive granite rock faces of Yosemite beaming down at me, calling me to climb. The next day found me jumping out of the van to say hello to every wildflower that dared to exist in the desert lands around Joshua Tree. Every scene blurring and warping together like melting postcards, with my blissful face in the middle.

The months continued to spiral into immeasurable beauty and wonder, taking us from beautiful national parks and forests to a small agricultural town in southern Oregon, where we worked on a hemp farm alongside other nomads. When the Alameda wildfire burned down the entire town, we stayed put even though we could've hopped in the van to chase clearer skies. We wanted to be with our friends. Community love and a protective nature develops quickly among those who remember their wandering roots, and have known what it feels like

to be truly alone out there. And building a community, especially with other BIPOC (Black, Indigenous and people of colour) and underrepresented nomads became an unexpected cornerstone of my vanlife identity: we'd gather together in hubs after periods of solitude.

All in a year, I shed preconceived notions of what a home or a successful family unit should look like. I became a drifter who made fast friends with anyone I met at a rest area or trailhead, because I felt we were all on the same journey of going very far just to discover what home means. I also discovered secrets to optimising the modern nomadic life experience, and maintaining a steady balance of remote freelance work with seasonal farm gigs that allowed to us connect deeply with the Earth's changes.

My name means 'wanderer' (thank you, mum and dad). I am still learning what that means to me, and what wandering can bring.

"WE NEED THE TONIC
AT THE SAME TIME THAT
TO EXPLORE AND
WE REQUIRE THAT ALL
AND UNEXPLORABLE
SEA BE INDEFINITELY
AND UNFATHOMED
UNFATHOMABLE. WE
ENOUGH OF

OF WILDNESS...
WE ARE EARNEST
LEARN ALL THINGS,
THINGS BE MYSTERIOUS
THAT LAND AND
WILD, UNSURVEYED
BY US BECAUSE
CAN NEVER HAVE
NATURE."

– HENRY DAVID THOREAU, WALDEN

CLIMB EVERY MOUNTAIN

Start summiting the world's mountains and you might find it a hard habit to kick. Striking out each day, your pack filled with waterproofs, food and water, plus a compass and a map (and the wherewithal to use them), you make your way up to the curved head of a valley. The walk gets tougher now, becoming more of scramble, then a balancing act along a ridge. But up here the views are staggering. And so is the wind. You hug the rock at the summit, limpet-like, before turning round, exhilarated.

1

Corbetts
Scotland, UK

A Munro is any hill in Scotland that is more than 914m (3000ft) high; they're not a single range but rather a collection named after a list kept by Sir Hugh Munro in the 19th century. Daunted by the number and altitude of the Munros? Then perhaps start peak-bagging with the Corbetts, which is the collective name for Scottish hills from 762m to 9842m (2500ft to 3000ft) in height. There are just 221 of them.

Essential information:
Bunk down in a frugal bothy (overnight hut) with the unforgettable rewards of sweeping views and fireside camaraderie.

2

Fourteeners
USA

Colorado and California are home to most of the peaks in the US higher than 4270m (14,000ft), though the highest is 6190m (2300ft) Denali in Alaska. Ticking off Colorado's 53 fourteeners is a popular pastime for climbers, and there are plenty of delightful small towns and unique adventures to experience along the way. Longs Peak attracts significant attention from non-professional climbers, with around 15,000 attempted summits every year.

Essential information:
While not technical, Longs Peak is a gruelling 20km (12-mile) slog requiring a 3am start, and has a success rate of less than 50%.

3

The Aussie 8
Australia

To scale the highest peak in each of Australia's eight states, you won't be climbing higher than 2228m/7310ft (that's Mt Kosciuszko in New South Wales' Snowy Mountains) – but you will be journeying vast distances between them. Kosciuszko is a memorable ascent; you'll be accessing expansive views of boulder-strewn plateaus and hills where gum trees cling on for dear life.

Essential information:
In the 'Snowies' skiers arrive from early June to late August; it's probably best to avoid the winter peak season if hiking here, though it's still accessible at this time.

4

Eight-thousanders
Nepal, China, India
& Pakistan

Of the Earth's 14 peaks higher than 8000m (26,247ft), the most famed is Mt Everest; the others are also in the Himalaya and the Karakoram. Summit them all and you'll join an exclusive club of 45 climbers, including Nirmal 'Nims' Purja, who conquered all 14 over seven months in 2019, and later launched the Great Mountain Cleanup campaign to remove waste from Himalaya peaks.

Essential information:
The 'easiest' of the 14 is Cho Oyu: the most common ascent route is the northwest ridge through the Chinese Base Camp.

Clockwise, from top: wildflowers below USA fourteener Mt Rainier; gear up and get out on the mountain trails; overnight camp in the Karakoram, Pakistan

GOING HOME

Stephanie Pearson finds her family's roots in Minnesota

We humans are restless. More than a billion international travellers cross borders annually, while one in 30 of us live outside our country of origin. The urge to migrate seems embedded in our collective DNA. With so much frenetic motion, 'home' can just as easily signify the cloud where we store our Instagrams as it can a physical address or a country of origin.

I'm a 4th-generation American. In 1883, my great-grandfather, Peter Pearson, left the village of Tvååker, Sweden, to start a new life in the mining and logging boomtown of Tower, Minnesota. Legend had it that on this frozen frontier, the Norway pines were so tall they blocked out the sun.

In the spring of 1909 my great-grandfather, his wife Josephine – also a Swedish immigrant – and their nine children moved into a farmhouse, 16km (10 miles) south of Tower. The house was 6m by 8m (20ft by 20ft), a storey and a half, and built on wooden blocks, with a kitchen, dining room and living room downstairs, and one giant, low-ceilinged bedroom upstairs.

'On the cold winter nights, to keep from freezing, it was necessary to sleep in our long woollen underwear, plus German socks which extended over one's knees', my great-uncle Morrie wrote in his diary. 'There was no ceiling upstairs and the roof was not insulated, the rafters were visible and white with frost. When the temperature got down to -40°F, the jack-pine logs in the walls boomed like a rifle shot as they cracked open.' The summer was short, but the giant garden would still produce potatoes,

cabbage, lettuce, carrots, squash and raspberries. In late June the field to the east would bloom with thousands of daisies, buttercups and prairie-fire flowers.

'On nice, warm sunny Sundays,' Morrie wrote, 'the family would pack a picnic basket and follow a narrow path to the crest of the hill where we would sit on the ground and enjoy the most delicious food ever served, listening to the birds and the wind playing a tune through the needles of the pine trees. Their pungent fragrance added to the taste of the food.'

More than a century later, I live in Santa Fe, New Mexico, 2414km (1500 miles) to the south. But my parents still spend summers on a lake 48km (30 miles) from the old family homestead. When I visit them in late June, I ride my bike to the farmhouse. It's a wreck. Falling in on itself and infested with mice, it's been condemned as a fire hazard. But if I time my visit correctly, the blooming buttercups, the daisies and the prairie-fire still overtake the adjoining field.

I often dream of tearing down the farmhouse, erecting a modern, light-filled cabin, and re-rooting the Pearson name to this place. It's an irrational impulse. The farm was never my own home and I visited my great-uncle Arnold, who took it over from my great-grandfather, only a few times a year as a child. Northern Minnesota is the antithesis of progressive or exotic, but it is the place where I still feel a tangible link to my family's past. And, for me, that makes it one of the most desirable destinations in this wide, restless world.

SOW SOME SEEDS

By taking part in one of the many tree-planting schemes worldwide or by purchasing your very own parcel of Amazonian rainforest, you can sow seeds – literally. But metaphorically, this is about the adage 'you get out of life what you put into it'. As they say in Australia, from little things, big things grow.

SAVE A LIFE

Changes you make in your daily life can impact lives around the world. Frequently, in places like Sarawak, Malaysia, deforestation affects living creatures like the orangutan, causing many orphans. Deciding not to buy products that exacerbate environmental degradation helps save lives (the paper in Lonely Planet's books is all ethically sourced).

JOIN A RESEARCH EXPEDITION

There were people on the HMS *Beagle* besides just Charles Darwin, you know. Take a journey of discovery – scientific discovery – by joining a research expedition to a far-flung corner of the world. You don't need a PhD, just enthusiasm and the willingness to take samples, label containers or sit by a computer entering info. Why simply hike when you could also be logging data about endangered trees? Why just snorkel when you could also be taking coral samples to track reef health? Bring your curiosity and sense of adventure, and both you and the world will benefit.

1

US Antarctic Program
Antarctica

Each year, the US Antarctic Program sends about 3000 people to work at research bases on the world's southernmost continent. Non-scientists are needed as support staff: carpenters, bakers, electricians, machine operators and more. Jobs usually last through austral summer – October to February – when the stations are accessible by plane. The largest facility is McMurdo Station, on the south tip of Ross Island, where orcas, seals and penguins frolic in frigid waters offshore.

Essential information:
Apply to work at Antarctic research stations via the United States' National Science Foundation website.

Far left to right: green turtle at Ningaloo Reef; collect research data in Peru's Cordillera Blanca; sign up for a stint at McMurdo Station with the US Antarctic Program

2

Adventure Scientists
USA

This Montana-based organisation is always looking for outdoorsy types to help with timber tracking – creating databases of leaf, seed and wood samples to monitor tree-species numbers and help curb illegal logging. Volunteers might hike southern Appalachian forests or Maryland's eastern shores in search of eastern white oak; or track glorious hardwoods – a common victim of timber theft – in northern Michigan. Other projects are in the works across the country.

Essential information:
Adventure Scientists has regular volunteer sign-ups via their website.

3

Ningaloo Turtle Program
Australia

Australia is home to six out of the seven species of sea turtle, and local communities rely on volunteers to monitor and protect the animals during nesting season. At Western Australia's Ningaloo Reef, volunteers wake at dawn to walk the beaches in search of eggs and ward off predators like foxes. You might be asked to camp on a remote beach to monitor nesting sites, or to join in a turtle rescue. Cool off with a dip in the vodka-clear Pacific – then do it all over again.

Essential information:
The turtles come to nest on the beaches of Ningaloo Reef between November and March.

4

American Alpine Institute
Peru

Up in Peru's Parque Nacional Huascarán, AAI volunteers (rock-climbers are especially welcome) head into the craggy Cordillera Blanca to scale glaciated peaks and trek alpine valleys, gathering information on air pollution, animal grazing, insect populations, water quality and more. Wake in a tent to frigid high-altitude mornings, sipping coffee beneath snowy peaks before heading off on a day of data collection, keeping eyes peeled for vicunas, condors and spectacled bears.

Essential information:
Trip length depends on the number of segments you choose to undertake: either 11, 21, 30, 41 or 48 days.

A PHOTO
A DAY

Chronicle your year and all your adventures
– far and near – by taking a photo a day and
saving them all in one place (several online
communities allow this). For enthusiastic
photographers it's a good discipline to observe.
And at the end of the year, when you look back
through the shots, expect to laugh, cry and be
surprised at the memories attached to them.

"ALL LIVING
A MEASURE OF
MOVES THEM IN
INEXPLICABLE WAYS.
CAN BE SAVING; IT
OF THE ABILITY TO
NO SPECIES

THINGS CONTAIN MADNESS THAT STRANGE, SOMETIMES THIS MADNESS IS PART AND PARCEL ADAPT. WITHOUT IT, WOULD SURVIVE."

– YANN MARTEL, *LIFE OF PI*

HIT THE ROAD

Nothing helps us connect with the real world like travel. No matter if you're taking a bus in Dakar, Senegal or catching the Metro in Paris, travel is always an opportunity to discover new places and people. See where serendipity takes you.

PHOTO CREDITS

INDEX

NOTES

YOU ONLY LIVE ONCE

You Only Live Once 2nd edition
March 2023
Published by Lonely Planet Global Limited
CRN 554153
www.lonelyplanet.com
2 3 4 5 6 7 8 9 10
Printed in Malaysia
ISBN 978 18386 9602 3
© Lonely Planet 2023
© photographers as indicated 2023

Written by Sarah Barrell, Robin Barton, David Cornthwaite, Mya-Rose Craig, Maggie Downs, Dan Fahey, Sunny Fitzgerald, Emily Frost, Ben Handicott, Anita Isalska, India Latham, Travis Levius, Emily Matchar, Shafik Meghji, Tracey Minkin, Stephanie Pearson, Monisha Rajesh, Faren Rajkumar, Adam Skolnick, Kamala Thiagarajan, Holly Tuppen, Christina Webb, Nicola Williams

General Manager, Publishing: Piers Pickard

Associate Publisher: Robin Barton

Commissioning Editor: Christina Webb

Editor: Polly Thomas

Illustrations: Holly Exley

Maps: Wayne Murphy

Print Production: Nigel Longuet

All rights reserved. No part of this publication may be reproduced, stored in a retrieval system or transmitted in any form by any means, electronic, mechanical, photocopying, recording or otherwise except brief extracts for the purpose of review, without the written permission of the publisher. Lonely Planet and the Lonely Planet logo are trademarks of Lonely Planet and are registered in the US patent and Trademark Office and in other countries.

Lonely Planet Global Ltd Office

Digital Depot, Roe Lane (off Thomas St), Digital Hub, Dublin 8, D08 TCV4 Ireland

STAY IN TOUCH
lonelyplanet.com/contact
Although the authors and Lonely Planet have taken all reasonable care in preparing this book, we make no warranty about the accuracy or completeness of its content and, to the maximum extent permitted, disclaim all liability from its use.

Paper in this book is certified against the Forest Stewardship Council™ standards. FSC™ promotes environmentally responsible, socially beneficial and economically viable management of the world's forests.